Traditional American Cookery

Beryl MacDonald

Traditional American Cookery

CASSELL
LONDON

CASSELL & CO LTD.
35 Red Lion Square, London WC1 R 4SG
and at Sydney, Auckland, Toronto, Johannesburg,
an affiliate of
Macmillan Publishing Co., Inc.,
New York.

First published 1978

ISBN 0 304 29914 6

Typeset by Inforum Limited, Portsmouth
Printed in Great Britain by
Fletcher & Son Ltd, Norwich
Bound by Richard Clay (The Chaucer Press) Ltd,
Bungay, Suffolk

Contents

Acknowledgements

My special thanks go to my friend Terris Jones in London, who was very helpful to me in determining the availability of food items in Britain. My thanks also to my husband John, and our many friends, who were my guinea-pigs during the testing of recipes contained in this book.

Beryl MacDonald

Author's Note

Most of the ingredients mentioned in this book are readily available in the British Isles. A few will not be found in all food shops but can be purchased in some department store grocery sections, or in speciality grocery shops.

All spices used are powdered and all herbs powdered or crushed, unless otherwise specified: eg. *stick* cinnamon, *whole* cloves, etc.

Measurements for recipes are given in both British Imperial and Metric (in italics), but they are *not* exact equivalents and the cook is advised to keep to one set of measurements to be sure of correct proportions. In some instances no reference is made to either type of measurement, eg. *1 small onion* or *two eggs*, and in many sandwich and cocktail recipes. Where a measurement (eg. 1¾ tsp) is given only in the Imperial column, it means that the Metric equivalent is identical

Approximate Conversions

```
       2.2 lb  =  1 kg
         1 lb  =  450 gm
         1 oz  =   30 gm

 1 qt (2 pt)   =  1,200 ml
        1¾ pt  =  1 l. (1000 ml)
         1 pt  =  575 ml
1 gill (¼ pt)  =  150 ml

        1 tbsp =  15 ml
         1 tsp =   5 ml
```

Glossary

Barbecued   cooked on a barbecue grill; *also* any food cooked or served in barbecue sauce, such as Oven Barbecued Chicken, Barbecued Ham Sandwich

Beet   Beetroot

Biscuit   a small roll, similar to a scone but not sweet

Blueberry   bilberry

Candy   sweets

Chowder   a type of soup, usually containing meat or fish and vegetables

Cobbler   a type of fruit pie with top crust only

Conserve   type of jam, usually with nuts included

Cookies   sweet biscuits, sometimes cake-like, such as Brownies

Corn Meal   meal made from maize or sweet corn, usually yellow; *not* corn-flour

Frijoles   beans (Spanish)

Frijoles Refritos   beans, refried

Frosting   icing, as on cake

Molasses   treacle, *not* golden syrup

Pie   pie *except* when it is Boston Cream Pie, Ozark Pie, Washington Pie: all of which are cakes

Pudding   pudding, but also includes custards and blancmanges

Shortcake   a type of scone, usually eaten with fruit e.g. Strawberry Shortcake

Zucchini   courgettes

Introduction

It takes more than miles to measure the distance between a Maine Lobster and a Hawaiian pineapple, or between Alaskan Bear Stew and fresh-squeezed Florida orange juice. Distances are great in the United States of America, but just as great are the differences between the various types of cuisine which go together to make up American cooking.

The food supply is as varied as the climate and terrain. Thousands of miles of coastline yield oysters, crabs, clams and lobsters. From Alaskan waters comes the giant Chinook salmon. There are coconuts from Hawaii, peanuts from Alabama, grapefruit from Arizona, and beef and corn from the Central Plains region. California produces lettuce and tomatoes for salad, and grapes for wine. Apples, pears and cherries are grown in the valleys of Oregon and Washington.

Today, giant canneries and frozen food plants preserve the local produce, and jet planes and refrigerated vehicles carry food fresh from fields and orchards, as well as canned and frozen foods, to all parts of the country. Minnesotans may breakfast on fresh Hawaiian papayas (paw-paws) with a squeeze of lime juice, while San Franciscans dine on Kansas beefsteak. It was not always so.

People came to America from all parts of the world. They adapted the recipes of the old lands to fit the harvest of the new. Cooking took on a regional flavour. Special dishes grew around special holidays. As the wagon trains carried the people westward, cooking traditions went with them, but the recipes often had to be adapted to suit the food which could be carried in the wagons, and adapted again at the end of the trail.

Three hundred years have blended the peoples and the cultures. There are new methods of cooking, and new recipes are invented constantly. Nevertheless, Boston Baked Beans are still Boston Baked Beans even when they are baked in Los Angeles, and the old recipes are preserved along with the new. That is the tradition of American cooking.

PART I

People, Places and Occasions

The American Indians

THE COUNTRY'S FIRST COOKS

When the first white people arrived in North America they found in the American Indians more than one cultural group. Although racially linked, the Indians were and are many nations, their cultures as varied as the regions in which they live.

The Indians of the Southwest were primarily agricultural and lived in permanent villages. Their houses were built of adobe (sun-dried clay) and they grew corn and beans and peppers, as well as cotton which they wove into cloth. They had domesticated the wild turkey.

When Lewis and Clark were led by the Indian girl Sacajawea into the Pacific Northwest, they found many tribes congregated along the rivers where they fished for salmon and trout. There were bears and deer and elk to be hunted, and huckleberries and salmonberries grew abundantly. Coastal Indians built dugout canoes, sometimes forty feet long, in which they put out to sea to fish for halibut and to hunt for whales. The homes of the Northwest Indians were large and built of cedar planks.

The Indians of the Great Plains were nomads. They followed the great buffalo herds which supplied their food, as well as hides for their moccasins, robes and coverings for the tepees in which they lived. In the Southeast, homes had thatched roofs, quite different from the wigwams and longhouses of the Northeast.

Eventually the European settlers spread their culture across the continent, but many aspects of Indian culture are woven through the civilization of the United States. The paths over which the Indians travelled were the trails followed by the wagon trains; they eventually became the modern highways of today. Indian languages are perpetuated in the names of most of the states and many cities and rivers. Names like Massachusetts and Alabama, Pocatello and Waukesha; Okefenokee, Clackamas and Clatskanie.

Indian ways of preparing food formed the basis for much of American cookery. It was the Indian woman who first cooked the native foods, seasoning them with wild herbs. Early colonial settlers, confronted with the strange foods, adopted the Indian recipes. Many of those recipes survive today. The peppers and beans of the Southwest Indians were, and still are, made into soups, chillis, and barbecue sauces. The Mexican cooking of that region is more Indian than Spanish in origin. Indians knew potatoes, tomatoes and sweet corn; peanuts, peppers and avocadoes; pineapple, vanilla, cocoa and maple sugar. It was they who invented the popcorn which Americans munch when they go to the movies. Even the Clambake, a New England speciality, was Indian in origin.

A few recipes are listed here, but American Indian cooking and influence are all through this book.

INDIAN BEAN SOUP

200 gm .	8 oz	dried haricot beans
1 l. .	1 qt	water
	1	onion, chopped
	2	tomatoes, peeled and chopped
50 gm .	2 oz	salt pork, diced
1¾ tsp .	2 tsp	chilli powder
1¼ tsp .	1½ tsp	salt
1¼ l. .	2½ pt	water

Soak beans in 1 qt (1 l.) cold water for 3 hours. Drain, rinse and drain again. Add onion, tomatoes, pork and seasonings and 2½ pt (1¼ l.) water and mix well. Simmer, covered, for 1½ hours. Uncover and continue cooking, stirring occasionally, for 45 minutes, adding more water if necessary.

Serves 4 — 6.

SQUASH WITH ONIONS

900 gm .	2 lb	marrow or courgettes
	10	spring onions, chopped
	1 tsp	salt
	¼ tsp	pepper
	¼ tsp	marjoram
50 gm .	2 oz	melted butter

Peel and slice marrow ¼ in. (6 mm) thick. Combine with onions and seasonings in ovenproof dish. Pour butter over the surface, cover dish and bake in a moderate oven (350°F, 180°C, Gas Mark 4) for 2 hours.

Serves 6.

BEANS WITH GREEN PEPPERS

25 gm .	1 oz	streaky bacon, diced
	½	green pepper, diced
	½	onion, chopped
	1 clove	garlic, crushed
	2	tomatoes, chopped
	1 tsp	sugar

⅛ tsp	nutmeg
¼ tsp	salt
dash	pepper
450 gm . 1 lb	tinned red kidney beans

Fry bacon with green pepper, onion and garlic 5 minutes. Add tomatoes, sugar, nutmeg, salt and pepper and simmer 10 minutes. Add beans and pour into an ovenproof dish. Bake in a moderate oven (350° F, 180° C, Gas Mark 4) for 30 minutes.
Serves 4.

STEWED TOMATOES, INDIAN STYLE

900 gm . 2 lb	tomatoes
1	onion, finely chopped
1 stick	celery, chopped
1 tsp	salt
⅛ tsp	pepper
3 tbsp	dry breadcrumbs

Peel tomatoes and cut into small chunks. Combine with onion, celery, salt and pepper and simmer 10 minutes. Gradually stir in breadcrumbs and simmer 5 minutes.
Serves 6.

SUCCOTASH

250 gm . 10 oz	frozen sweet corn
250 gm . 10 oz	frozen lima beans or broad beans
1 tbsp	butter
¼ tsp	salt
¼ tsp	pepper

Cook corn and beans separately until tender. Drain. Combine vegetables with butter, salt and pepper and mix lightly.
Serves 6 — 8.

INDIAN FRY BREAD

400 gm . 1 lb	plain flour
12 gm . ½ oz	sugar
1¾ tsp . 2 tsp	salt
5 tsp . 2 tbsp	baking powder
330 ml . ⅔ pt	lukewarm milk
2 tbsp	lukewarm water
1 tsp	butter

Mix flour, sugar, salt and baking powder together. Combine milk, water and butter and stir until butter is melted. Stir into flour mixture. Pinch off pieces of dough and flatten between the hands into 'cakes'. Fry in hot deep fat (325°F, 170°C) until golden-brown. Serve hot.

OVEN-BAKED   *150 gm* . 6 oz   plain flour
BREAD   ¾ tsp   baking powder
                           ¾ tsp   salt
             165 ml . ⅓ pt   water

Combine flour, baking powder and salt and stir in water. Spread in a well-greased 7-in. (18-cm) pie plate and bake in a moderately hot oven (400°F, 200°C, Gas Mark 6) for 25 minutes. Cut into wedges and serve immediately with butter.

HASTY   *550 ml* . 1 pt   boiling water
PUDDING   *100 gm* . 3½ oz   yellow cornmeal
                       ½ tsp   salt
            185 ml . ⅓ pt   cold water

Mix cornmeal and salt with the cold water and stir slowly into the boiling water. Cook over direct heat, stirring, for 3 minutes. Continue cooking in top of double saucepan, over simmering water, for 20 minutes. Pan should be covered during cooking. Serve hot with syrup or honey.

JOHNNY CAKES   *125 gm* . 5 oz   yellow cornmeal
                      ¾ tsp   salt
                      1 tsp   sugar
            250 ml . ½ pt   boiling water
            65 ml . ½ gill   milk

Mix cornmeal, salt and sugar. Pour boiling water over gradually and mix well. Stir in milk. Drop by tablespoonfuls onto a hot greased griddle or frying pan and fry until well browned on both sides. Serve immediately with butter and syrup or honey.

Serves 4 — 6.

CHILLI DIP

2	onions, minced
1 clove	garlic, crushed
2 tbsp	bacon drippings or butter
1 tbsp	plain flour
4	tomatoes, peeled and chopped
140 ml . 1 gill	water
1 tsp	sugar
¾ tsp	salt
2 tbsp	chilli powder
dash	cayenne pepper
¼ tsp	basil
1 tbsp	lemon juice

Fry onion and garlic in bacon fat until tender. Stir in flour. Add remaining ingredients, mix well, and simmer 20 minutes. Cool. Serve as a dip for crisp raw vegetables (carrots, celery, radishes, etc.) or with potato crisps.

New England

SEASHORE AND SKI SLOPE

In 1614, English explorer Captain John Smith named the area New England. The first pilgrims landed there at Plymouth Rock in 1620 and the English colony, struggling against and almost succumbing to the rocky soil and long, cold winters, flourished. Today, there are six individual states: Maine, Vermont, Massachusetts, New Hampshire, Connecticut, and Rhode Island. The descendants of the early English colonists are mingled with the descendants of nineteenth-century immigrants who came by the thousands from French-speaking Canada and Ireland, and, to a lesser extent, from every country in Europe. Yet the name New England persists.

Only one of the six states, Vermont, has no coastline, and the sea has always influenced New England life. The abundance of fish and shellfish helped to save the lives of the early colonists, and today it sustains the large commercial fishing industry and the modern plants where fish is canned and frozen, to be shipped across the continent. Maine lobsters are flown live to be cooked in San Francisco and other large cities where gourmets are willing to pay the cost.

Along the coast, throughout the summer, there are yacht races and regattas and fishing derbies. In Maine there is a Lobster Festival. The sea breezes lure New Yorkers away from the city's summer heat.

In land-locked Vermont, early spring means 'sugaring off' and the sap from the sugar maple trees is collected, to be turned into maple syrup and maple sugar candy. In the summer, there are Maple Sugar parties. Autumn brings tourists for the Fall Foliage Tours as the green leaves turn to fiery reds, oranges and yellows in one of nature's most flamboyant displays.

Winter is long and cold and the snow is deep. There are Winter Carnivals and ski races, and a Sled Dog Derby in New Hampshire. It will be a long time until summer and seashore Clambakes.

At a New England Clambake, a large pit is dug in the sand and stones are piled into the bottom. A fire is then built in the pit and the ashes are swept away from the hot rocks. Seaweed, clams, more seaweed, whole potatoes and sweet potatoes, ears of sweet corn and whole fish and lobsters, go into the pit in layers. A covering of wet canvas and still more seaweed go over the top and the food is cooked and flavoured by steam from the wet seaweed and heat from the rocks. The meal begins with bowls of steaming clam chowder or codfish chowder and then the pit is uncovered. The clams are taken from their shells and dipped in melted butter. The succulent lobsters and baked fish are unearthed, to be eaten with the potatoes and corn. Cups of steaming coffee go along with the blueberry pies and blackberry cobblers.

Even without a handy pit, or even a handy seashore, the Clambake, or a reasonable facsimile of it, can be prepared in an ordinary kitchen.

NEW ENGLAND CLAM CHOWDER			
150 gm .	6 oz	salt pork, diced
	2	onions, chopped
400 gm .	1 lb	potatoes, peeled and diced
	2 dozen	clams, with juice
1¾ tsp .	2 tsp	salt
	½ tsp	pepper
750 ml .	1½ pt	milk

Fry salt pork until golden-brown. Add onion and cook until tender. Drain off most of fat. Add potatoes, juice from clams, salt and pepper and simmer, covered, until potatoes are tender. Chop clams very finely and add to mixture. Simmer, covered, 10 minutes. Add milk and heat. Serve with crackers.
Serves 8.

FISH CHOWDER			
450 gm .	1 lb	white fish, such as cod or haddock
550 ml .	1 pt	water
	1 tsp	salt
450 gm .	1 lb	potatoes, diced
50 gm .	2 oz	salt pork, diced
	1	onion, chopped
	2 tbsp	plain flour
550 ml .	1 pt	milk

Put fish, water and salt in a saucepan and simmer gently until fish can be flaked with a fork. Remove fish from water, discard skin and bones and strain broth. Cook potatoes in fish broth until tender. Fry salt pork and onion together until tender. Stir in flour and gradually add milk. Add broth and cook, stirring, until thickened. Add fish, potatoes, and salt and pepper to taste.
Serves 6.

STEAMED CLAMS

Allow a dozen clams per person. Scrub shells with a soft brush. Place on rack in steamer with small amount of water and steam until shells open. Discard clams which do not open. Serve in heated bowls with small cups of melted butter for dipping.

BAKED SWEET POTATOES

Select equal-sized sweet potatoes, about 8 oz (225 gm) each. Scrub skins with stiff brush and pierce in several places with sharp knife. Rub skins lightly with oil and bake in moderate oven (350°F, 180°C, Gas Mark 4) until tender (60-75 minutes). Cut cross in top of each sweet potato and squeeze open. Place a pat of butter on top.

BAKED POTATOES

Select equal-sized potatoes, about 10 oz (280 gm) each. Do not use new potatoes. Scrub skins with stiff brush and pierce in several places with sharp knife. Bake in a moderately hot oven (400°F, 200°C, Gas Mark 6) until tender (about 1 hour). For softer skins, rub skins lightly with cooking oil before baking.

Note: Potatoes may be baked in a moderate oven (350°F, 180°C, Gas Mark 4) for about 90 minutes.

CORN ON THE COB

4 ears	very fresh sweet corn
2 tsp	salt
	boiling water

Remove husks and silk from corn and place in a large saucepan. Cover with boiling water, add salt, and simmer 6 minutes. Serve with butter.

BAKED FISH FILLETS

1 kg .	2½ lb	sole fillets
		salt and pepper
3½ tsp .	4 tsp	lemon juice
50 gm .	2 oz	cracker crumbs
	4	spring onions, chopped
2½ tbsp .	3 tbsp	chopped parsley
	½ tsp	salt

```
          ¼ tsp    pepper
100 gm .  4 oz    bacon, cut in half
                  slices
```

Sprinkle fillets with salt, pepper and lemon juice and lay them in a buttered ovenproof dish. Mix next five ingredients and sprinkle over fish. Lay bacon over top and bake in a moderately hot oven (400°F, 200°C, Gas Mark 6) for 30 minutes. Lift fillets onto platter.

Serves 6.

SEAFOOD
NEWBERG

```
3½ tbsp .  4 tbsp   butter
2½ tbsp .  3 tbsp   flour
 375 ml .  ¾ pt     milk
           ½ tsp    salt
           ¼ tsp    pepper
           ¼ tsp    nutmeg
              3     egg yolks, beaten
3½ tbsp .  4 tbsp   dry sherry
 200 gm .  ½ lb     cooked lobster, in
                    small chunks
 200 gm .  ½ lb     cooked shelled shrimps
```

Melt butter and stir in flour. Gradually stir in milk, add salt, pepper and nutmeg, and cook over low heat, stirring continually, until mixture thickens. Stir a small amount of hot sauce into egg yolks then stir slowly back into sauce. Continue stirring and cooking for one minute. Add sherry, lobster and shrimps, and continue cooking, stirring very gently, for 5 minutes. Serve over toast.

Serves 4 — 6.

Variations: Substitute other cooked seafood or fish such as crab, tuna, sea scallops, or a combination.

NEW ENGLAND
BOILED
DINNER

```
2½ kg .  4-5 lb    salt beef or silverside
450 gm .  1 lb     small whole onions, peeled
675 gm .  1½ lb    small carrots, scraped
675 gm .  1½ lb    small whole potatoes,
                   peeled
           1       turnip, chopped
675 gm .  1½ lb    cabbage, quartered
```

Cover beef with cold water, bring to boil and simmer until tender (about 2½ hours). Add onions, turnip, and carrots and simmer 30 minutes. Add potatoes and cabbage and simmer 30 minutes. Lift meat and vegetables onto a warm platter.

Serves 8.

RED FLANNEL HASH	2 tbsp . 2 tbsp	butter
	1	onion, chopped
	150 gm . 6 oz	cooked beetroot, chopped
	1 large	potato, cooked and chopped
	225 gm . 8 oz	cooked boiled beef (or corned beef)
	½ tsp	salt
	¼ tsp	pepper

Melt butter and fry onion until tender. Add beetroot, potato. Mince the beef and add to vegetables with salt and pepper; mix well. Cook over low heat until lightly browned on the bottom.

Serves 4.

BOSTON BAKED BEANS	450 gm . 1 lb	haricot beans
	1 l. . 1 qt	cold water
	125 ml . 1 gill	treacle
	½ tsp . ½ tsp	mustard powder
	1 tsp	salt
	1 tbsp	brown sugar
	100 gm . 4 oz	salt pork, in one piece

Cover beans with cold water and soak overnight. Bring to boil and simmer until skins burst. Drain beans but do not discard liquid. Mix treacle, mustard powder, salt and brown sugar. Make several slashes in the salt pork but do not cut through the rind. Place beans in large ovenproof dish and push the piece of salt pork down into them so that only rind shows. Add ½ pint (275 ml) of the bean liquid to the treacle mixture and mix well. Pour over the beans and pour additional liquid until beans are covered. Cover dish and bake in a very slow oven (250°F, 120°C, Gas Mark 1) for six hours, removing cover for last hour of baking. Add extra liquid during baking if necessary.

Serves 6.

BOSTON BROWN BREAD	75 gm . 3 oz	plain flour
	90 gm . 3½ oz	yellow cornmeal
	75 gm . 3 oz	whole wheat flour
	1 tsp	salt
	1 tsp	bicarbonate of soda
	5 tsp . 2 tbsp	sugar
	50 gm . 2 oz	raisins
	140 ml . 1 gill	black treacle
	250 ml . ½ pt	buttermilk

Combine first seven ingredients. Mix treacle with buttermilk and add to flour mixture. Wash and grease three 1-lb (450-gm) size fruit or vegetable tins. Pour batter into tins and cover tightly with foil. Stand upright in a steamer, add water and steam for 3 hours. Serve warm with butter.

CORN MUFFINS

100 gm .	4 oz	yellow cornmeal
100 gm .	4 oz	plain flour
3 tsp .	3½ tsp	baking powder
5 tsp .	2 tbsp	sugar
	½ tsp	salt
	1	egg
190 ml .	1½ gills	milk
50 gm .	2 oz	cooking fat, melted

Combine dry ingredients. Beat egg and combine with milk and melted fat. Pour into cornmeal mixture and stir only until mixed. Batter will be lumpy. Spoon into greased patty tins, two-thirds full, and bake in a moderately hot oven (425°F, 220°C, Gas Mark 7) until golden-brown (about 25 minutes). Serve immediately with butter.
12 muffins.

BLUEBERRY PIE

550 gm .	1¼ lb	bilberries
140 gm .	5 oz	sugar
	3 tbsp	plain flour
		shortcrust pastry for
		double-crust pie

Combine berries, sugar and flour and mix well. Prepare pastry and use half to line a 9-in. (23-cm) pie plate. Pour in berry mixture. Cover with top crust. Seal and crimp edges and prick top with a fork in several places. Bake in a hot oven (450°F, 230°C, Gas Mark 8) for 10 minutes. Reduce heat (350°F, 180°C, Gas Mark 4) and bake until fruit begins to bubble (20-25 minutes). Sprinkle crust with sugar. Serve warm with vanilla ice cream.

BLACKBERRY COBBLER

400 gm .	1 lb	blackberries
100 gm .	4 oz	sugar
	1 tsp	lemon juice
2½ tsp .	1 tbsp	plain flour
125 gm .	5 oz	plain flour
½ tsp .	½ tsp	salt
1½ tsp .	1¾ tsp	baking powder
2½ tsp .	1 tbsp	sugar
2½ tbsp .	3 tbsp	salad oil
125 ml .	1 gill	milk

Combine first four ingredients in saucepan and cook, stirring, until mixture is thickened. Pour into ovenproof dish. Mix flour, salt, baking powder and sugar. Blend oil with milk and add to flour mixture. Mix well and drop by spoonfuls on to hot fruit. Bake in a moderately hot oven (400° F, 200°C, Gas Mark 6) until golden-brown (about 30 minutes). Serve with cream.
Serves 6.

HARVARD	600 gm . 1½ lb	fresh beetroots
BEETS	2½ tsp . 1 tbsp	cornflour
	1¾ tsp . 2 tsp	sugar
	½ tsp	salt
	125 ml . 1 gill	cooking liquid from beetroot, cooled
	65 ml . ½ gill	vinegar

Cook beetroots in water until tender. Drain, reserving 1 gill (125 ml) of liquid, peel and cut into cubes. Mix cornflour, sugar, salt and gradually stir in liquid and vinegar. Cook over low heat, stirring, until thickened. Add beetroot and heat.
Serves 4.

BLUEBERRY	175 gm . 7 oz	plain flour
MUFFINS	2½ tsp	baking powder
	¾ tsp	salt
	3 tbsp	sugar
	1	egg, beaten
	125 ml . 1 gill	milk
	4 tbsp	cooking oil
	125 gm . 5 oz	bilberries

Sieve together flour, baking powder, salt and sugar. Combine egg, milk and oil and add to flour mixture. Stir just until blended. Fold in bilberries gently and pour into greased patty tins (two-thirds full). Bake in a moderately hot oven (400°F, 200°C, Gas Mark 6) for 25 minutes.

BOSTON CREAM	150 gm . 6 oz	plain flour
PIE	200 gm . 8 oz	sugar
	1½ tsp . 1¾ tsp	baking powder
	½ tsp	salt
	190 ml . 1½ gills	milk
	75 gm . 3 oz	cooking fat
	1	egg

                    1 tsp   vanilla essence
                             Cream Filling
                             Chocolate Glaze

Blend dry ingredients. Mix milk, cooking fat, egg and vanilla and add to
flour mixture. Beat vigorously with wooden spoon or electric mixer for 3 or
4 minutes. Pour into two greased and floured 8-in. (20-cm) sandwich tins
and bake in a moderate oven (350°F, 180°C, Gas Mark 4) 25-30 minutes.
Layers will be thin. Cool in tins 10 minutes, remove carefully and cool completely. Spread Cream Filling between layers and top with Chocolate Glaze.
Do not ice the sides of the cake.

Cream Filling   50 gm . 2 oz   sugar
                        5 tsp . 2 tbsp   cornflour
                             pinch   salt
                                 1   egg yolk
                       330 ml . ⅔ pt   milk
                             1 tsp   vanilla essence

Combine sugar, cornflour and salt in saucepan. Add egg yolk and mix well.
Gradually stir in milk. Cook, stirring, over low heat until thick. Stir in
vanilla and cool completely. Use as filling for Boston Cream Pie or any layer
cake.

Chocolate Glaze   50 gm . 2 oz   semi-sweet chocolate
                      2½ tbsp . 3 tbsp   butter
                      100 gm . 4 oz   icing sugar
                           ½ tsp   vanilla essence
                          1-2 tbsp   hot water

Melt chocolate and butter together in top of double saucepan. Add sugar
and vanilla and blend well. Add hot water very gradually until mixture is of
spreading consistency.

WASHINGTON PIE

Prepare cake layers as for Boston Cream Pie. Spread blackberry jam
between layers and sprinkle icing sugar over the top.

BLUEBERRY BUCKLE

75 gm	.	3 oz	butter or margarine
150 gm	.	6 oz	sugar
		1	egg
200 gm	.	8 oz	plain flour
1¾ tsp	.	2 tsp	baking powder
		¼ tsp	salt
165 ml	.	⅓ pt	milk
200 gm	.	8 oz	bilberries

Topping

50 gm	.	2 oz	butter
75 gm	.	3 oz	sugar
50 gm	.	2 oz	plain flour
		½ tsp	ground cinnamon

Cream butter with sugar. Beat in egg. Mix flour, baking powder and salt and add to batter alternately with milk. Fold in berries and spread in 9-in. (23-cm) square baking tin. Blend butter, sugar, flour and cinnamon for topping and sprinkle over batter. Bake in a moderate oven (375° F, 190° C, Gas Mark 5) 30 minutes or until knife inserted comes out clean. Cut into squares and serve warm.

6 — 8 servings.

APPLE PANDOWDY

600 gm	.	1½ lb	cooking apples
150 gm	.	6 oz	brown sugar
		¼ tsp	cinnamon
		¼ tsp	nutmeg
		¼ tsp	salt
125 gm	.	5 oz	plain flour
165 ml	.	⅓ pt	water
1¾ tsp	.	2 tsp	baking powder
		¼ tsp	salt
3½ tbsp	.	4 tbsp	cooking oil
65 ml	.	½ gill	milk

Peel, core and slice apples and arrange in a buttered ovenproof dish. Mix brown sugar, spices, ¼ teaspoon salt and 3 tablespoons of the flour with the water and cook, stirring, over low heat until thick. Pour over the apples. Combine remaining flour with the baking powder and salt. Mix oil with milk and stir in. Spread mixture over apples and bake in a moderate oven (375° F, 190° C, Gas Mark 5) 40 minutes. Serve warm with cream or ice cream.

Serves 6.

BLUEBERRY GRUNT

250 gm .	10 oz	bilberries
100 gm .	4 oz	sugar
250 ml .	½ pt	water
200 gm .	8 oz	plain flour
3½ tsp .	4 tsp	baking powder
	¼ tsp	salt
2½ tbsp .	3 tbsp	cooking oil
65 ml .	½ gill	milk

Mix berries, sugar and water in large frying pan and bring to boil. Lower heat. Combine flour, baking powder and salt. Mix oil with milk and add to flour mixture. Drop dough by heaping tablespoonfuls into hot berry mixture. Cover pan and simmer 20 minutes. Serve hot with cream.
    Serves 8.

Blackberry Grunt
Use blackberries in place of bilberries.

INDIAN PUDDING

500 ml .	1 pt	hot milk
50 gm .	2 oz	yellow cornmeal
50 gm .	2 oz	sugar
	½ tsp	salt
	½ tsp	cinnamon
	½ tsp	nutmeg
	¼ tsp	ginger
65 ml .	½ gill	treacle
250 ml .	½ pt	cold milk

Pour hot milk over cornmeal, sugar, salt and spices and mix well. Cook, stirring, over low heat, or in top of double saucepan, until thick. Add treacle and mix well. Pour into buttered ovenproof dish. Pour the cold milk over the pudding but do not stir. Bake in a slow oven (300° F, 150°C, Gas Mark 2) for 1½ hours. Serve warm with cream or ice cream.
    Serves 4.

GREEN TOMATO PIE

		shortcrust pastry for double-crust pie
900 gm .	2 lb	green tomatoes
225 gm .	8 oz	sugar

¼ tsp	salt
¼ tsp	nutmeg
¼ tsp	cinnamon
4 tbsp	plain flour
2 tbsp	lemon juice
1 tbsp	butter

Prepare pastry and line a 9-in. (23-cm) pie plate, using half of it. Roll remaining pastry into circle for top, cutting several small slits in it.

Peel and chop tomatoes. Mix with sugar, salt, spices, flour and lemon juice and turn into pastry-lined plate. Dot with butter, cover with top crust, crimp edges and bake in a hot oven (450°F, 230°C, Gas Mark 8) for 10 minutes. Reduce heat (350°F, 180°C, Gas Mark 4) and bake 30 minutes.

SNICKER-DOODLES

100 gm . 4 oz	butter or margarine
125 gm . 5 oz	sugar
1	egg
125 gm . 5 oz	plain flour
½ tsp	bicarbonate of soda
1 tsp	cream of tartar
¼ tsp	salt
1 tbsp	sugar
1 tsp	cinnamon

Cream butter and sugar and beat in egg. Sieve flour with soda, cream of tartar and salt and add to butter mixture. Mix well. Mix 1 tablespoon of sugar with 1 teaspoon of cinnamon. Shape dough into walnut-sized balls and roll in sugar-cinnamon mixture. Place 2 in. (5 cm) apart on ungreased baking sheet and bake in a moderately hot oven (400°F, 200°C, Gas Mark 6) for 8-10 minutes.

CRANBERRY CONSERVE

450 gm . 1 lb	cranberries
100 gm . 4 oz	raisins
2	oranges
1	lemon (juice and grated rind)
900 gm . 2 lb	sugar
50 gm . 2 oz	chopped nuts

Peel oranges and chop up peel. Discard white pith and seeds and chop up oranges. Mix peel, orange pulp, lemon rind and juice with cranberries, raisins and sugar. Cook, stirring occasionally, until thick. Add nuts and pour into sterilized jars and seal.

TOMATO
PRESERVES

1¼ kg .	3 lb	ripe tomatoes
1 kg .	2½ lb	sugar
125 ml .	1 gill	lemon juice
	1 tsp	ginger
	¼ tsp	cinnamon
	¼ tsp	cloves

Combine all ingredients in large saucepan. Bring to boil and cook until thick, stirring occasionally. Pour into hot sterilized jars and seal.

The Thanksgiving Feast

HARVEST AND HOPE IN A NEW LAND

In 1620, the *Mayflower* set sail from England, carrying 102 people. Later that year, the small group set up a colony in New England. Unfortunately, they were ill-prepared for the bitterly cold New England winter. By spring, almost half of them had died. Learning from the Indians, they planted the Indian sweet corn, a type of maize. They dug for clams which were plentiful along the beaches, and fished for lobsters and cod. The harvest was excellent, and Governor William Bradford decreed that a feast of thanksgiving should be held.

Corn was picked for the feast. Ears of corn were boiled or roasted whole, to be eaten off the cob the way the Indians did. There was corn to be pounded to a meal and made into Johnny Cakes and Hasty Pudding, and corn to be 'popped' into popcorn (another Indian discovery). Some of the kernels were combined with beans for Indian Succotash. Besides the corn, there were wild geese and ducks, fish and shellfish, wild cranberries, blueberries and blackberries. The Indians came to the feast, bringing venison and wild turkeys. The feast lasted for three days.

In 1623, Governor Bradford decreed that 30 July be set aside as an official Thanksgiving Day. Eventually, the custom spread to other colonies and in 1863, President Abraham Lincoln proclaimed the national observance of Thanksgiving Day. Today, it is held on the fourth Thursday of November and is a bank holiday.

It is not likely that the pilgrims' dinner bore a very great resemblance to the gargantuan repast served in most American homes today. Their wild turkeys would have been scrawny by comparison with today's selectively bred birds. Certainly, the ease of preparation is much greater today. There are no fires to be tended, not even a wood stove to stoke, and even the cranberry sauce can be bought in jars or tins.

Different regions of the country have developed their own traditions for this special day. For some families, the dinner would not be complete without Creamed Onions or Chestnut Stuffing. Troy Pudding is a New England speciality. Even Sauerkraut is traditional Thanksgiving fare for some. However, the basic meal of stuffed turkey, cranberries, sweet potatoes, and pumpkin pie, is eaten in all of the fifty states.

ROAST TURKEY	5-7 kg . 12-15 lb	turkey, oven-ready
		stuffing (recipes following)
	100 gm . 4 oz	butter, melted
		salt

Sprinkle neck and body cavities lightly with salt. Pack some of the stuffing loosely into neck cavity and pull skin flap over it, securing it with a skewer. Stuff body cavity loosely with stuffing and pull skin flaps over it. Run several short skewers through and lace with twine, crossing ends of twine and tying legs together. Place turkey, breast up, on rack in large roasting tin and brush with melted butter. Cover roaster and bake in a very moderate oven (325°F, 170°C, Gas Mark 3) until legs of turkey can be moved very easily (4-6 hours). Cover should be removed during last hour of cooking to allow bird to brown. Remove skewers and twine and place bird on platter or carving board. Allow to stand 30 minutes before carving. Serve with Giblet Gravy and Cranberry Sauce.

Savoury Bread Stuffing	600 gm . 1½ lb	bread, cut into small cubes)
	1¼ tsp . 1½ tsp	salt
	¼ tsp	pepper
	1 tsp	thyme
	1¼ tsp . 1½ tsp	sage
	2 tbsp	chopped parsley
	100 gm . 4 oz	butter or margarine
	2	onions, chopped
	2 sticks	celery, finely chopped
	65 ml . ½ gill	water

Mix bread, salt, pepper, thyme, sage and parsley. Melt butter and fry onion and celery gently until tender. Add water and cook 5 minutes. Pour mixture over bread and seasonings and mix well.

Note: If bird will not hold all of the stuffing, place excess in buttered oven-proof dish, cover and refrigerate. Place in oven with turkey during last hour of cooking.

Chestnut Stuffing	400 gm . 1 lb	chestnuts, cooked and chopped
	400 gm . 1 lb	soft breadcrumbs
	1¼ tsp . 1½ tsp	salt
	¼ tsp	pepper
	1 tsp	thyme
	1 tsp	sage
	2 tbsp	chopped parsley

100 gm .	4 oz	butter or margarine
	1	onion, finely chopped
	1 stick	celery, finely chopped
125 ml .	1 gill	water

Melt butter and fry onion and celery gently until tender. Add water and simmer 5 minutes. Mix chestnuts and bread with salt, pepper, thyme, sage and parsley. Pour the liquid mixture over and mix thoroughly.

Oyster Stuffing

Follow recipe for Chestnut Stuffing but use 12 oz (300 gm) chopped oysters in place of chestnuts.

Cornbread Stuffing			
	300 gm .	12 oz	Corn Bread *(see p. 35)*
	300 gm .	12 oz	white bread cubes
		½ tsp	sage
		½ tsp	thyme
		1 tsp	salt
		¼ tsp	pepper
	450 gm .	1 lb	sausage meat
		2	onions, chopped
		2 sticks	celery, finely chopped

Combine crumbled corn bread, white bread, sage, thyme, salt and pepper. Fry sausage meat with onions and celery until brown and tender. Keep the meat broken up as it cooks. Combine the two mixtures.

GIBLET GRAVY

		liver, heart and
		gizzard of turkey
		water
	1 tsp	salt
250 ml .	½ pt	drippings and juices
		from roast turkey
100 gm .	4 oz	flour
		salt and pepper

Place liver, heart and gizzard in saucepan with water to cover and 1 teaspoon salt. Simmer gently, covered, until tender. Chop giblets into very fine pieces. Measure liquid and add water to make one qt (one l.). Stir flour into the drippings and gradually add the liquid. Add chopped giblets and cook, stirring, until thickened. Add salt and pepper to taste.

CRANBERRY	400 gm . 1 lb	cranberries
SAUCE	400 gm . 1 lb	sugar
	¼ tsp	salt
	250 ml . ½ pt	water

Combine in saucepan and bring to boil. Cook, stirring occasionally, 15 minutes. Serve warm or cold, with turkey, pork or ham.

CANDIED SWEET	800 gm . 2 lb	sweet potatoes
POTATOES	100 gm . 4 oz	brown sugar
	65 ml . ½ gill	water
	50 gm . 2 oz	butter

Boil sweet potatoes in skins until barely tender. Cool, peel and cut into thick slices. Place in an ovenproof dish. Heat brown sugar, water and butter together, stirring, until butter melts. Pour over the sweet potatoes. Bake in a moderate oven (350°F, 180°C, Gas Mark 4) 30 minutes, basting frequently with the syrup.
    Serves 6.

SWEET POTATO	1¼ kg . 3 lb	sweet potatoes, cooked
CASSEROLE		and mashed
	125 ml . 1 gill	orange juice
	50 gm . 2 oz	butter, melted
	1	egg, beaten
	50 gm . 2 oz	brown sugar
	1 tsp	salt
	75 gm . 3 oz	miniature marsh-
		mallows

Mix together all ingredients except marshmallows. Turn into a buttered ovenproof dish and sprinkle marshmallows over surface. Bake in a moderate oven (350°F, 180°C, Gas Mark 4) for 30 minutes, or until marshmallows are golden.
    Serves 6 — 8.

SWEET	900 gm . 2 lb	sweet potatoes
POTATOES IN	6 large	oranges, halved
ORANGE CUPS	75 gm . 3 oz	brown sugar
	½ tsp	cinnamon
	50 gm . 2 oz	butter
	½ tsp	salt
	12	large marshmallows

Cook sweet potatoes in skins in boiling water until tender. Cool, remove skins and mash. Squeeze orange halves on a juicer, removing all seeds. Mix 2 tablespoons juice with sweet potatoes, brown sugar, cinnamon, butter and salt. Pile mixture into orange halves and press a marshmallow into the top of each. Place them on a baking sheet and bake in a moderate oven (375°F, 190°C, Gas Mark 5) for 30 minutes.

Serves 12.

CREAMED	675 gm . 1½ lb	small onions
ONIONS	2 tbsp	butter
	2 tbsp	plain flour
	400 ml . ¾ pt	milk
	1 tsp	salt
	⅛ tsp	pepper

Peel onions and cook in salted boiling water (1 teaspoon salt) until barely tender. Drain and place in buttered ovenproof dish. Melt butter, stir in flour and gradually add milk, salt and pepper. Cook, stirring, over low heat until thickened. Pour over onions and bake in a moderate oven (375°F, 190°C, Gas Mark 5) for 30 minutes.

Serves 8.

STUFFED	6 sticks	crisp celery
CELERY		Pineapple-Cheese Filling
		or Cheddar Filling

Wash and trim celery. Cut into 3-in. (8-cm) lengths, and stuff each piece with cheese filling. Refrigerate.

Pineapple-Cheese	100 gm . 4 oz	cream cheese, softened
Filling	3½ tbsp . 4 tbsp	drained crushed pineapple
	2½ tsp . 1 tbsp	juice from pineapple

Mix until smooth and well blended.

Cheddar Filling	50 gm . 2 oz	Cheddar cheese, grated
	25 gm . 1 oz	soft butter
	½ tsp	Worcestershire sauce
	¼ tsp	mustard powder

Mix all ingredients together with fork until smooth.

MOULDED	2 packets	orange jelly
CRANBERRY	400 ml . ¾ pt	boiling water
SALAD	450 gm . 1 lb	cranberry sauce (tinned or homemade)
	225 gm . 8 oz	tinned crushed pineapple
	1 stick	celery, finely chopped

Pour boiling water over jelly and stir until completely dissolved. Add cranberry sauce and mix well. Chill until thick but not set. Stir in pineapple and celery and pour into a mould. Chill until firm (3-4 hours). Unmould onto a plate just before serving.
  Serves 10.

RAW	400 gm . 1 lb	raw cranberries
CRANBERRY	75 gm . 3 oz	sugar
SALAD	500 gm . 20 oz	tinned crushed pineapple
	400 gm . 1 lb	miniature marshmallows
	200 gm . 8 oz	chopped nuts
	250 ml . ½ pt	cream, stiffly whipped

Put berries through mincer and combine with sugar and pineapple. Refrigerate 12 hours. Add marshmallows and nuts; mix well. Gently stir in whipped cream until well blended. Pour into a large bowl and chill at least 2 hours.
  Serves 12.

CRANBERRY	450 gm . 1 lb	cranberry sauce (tinned or homemade)
SAUCE SALAD	450 gm . 1 lb	tinned crushed pineapple
	170 gm . 6 oz	miniature marshmallows
	100 gm . 4 oz	desiccated coconut

Mix all ingredients and refrigerate several hours.
  Serves 8.

PARKERHOUSE	7 gm . ¼ oz	active dry yeast
ROLLS	65 ml . ½ gill	warm water
	165 ml . ⅓ pt	milk, scalded
	50 gm . 2 oz	sugar
	1 tsp	salt
	1	egg, beaten
	2½ tbsp . 3 tbsp	salad oil
	450-500 gm . 18-20 oz	plain flour

Mix yeast and warm water and leave to stand 5 minutes. Add milk which has been cooled to lukewarm, sugar, salt, egg and oil. Add half of the flour and beat until smooth. Add more flour, a little at a time, until dough is stiff and not too sticky to handle. Put remaining flour on a board and turn the dough onto it. Knead well for 5-8 minutes, working in more of the flour only as required to prevent stickiness. Place doughball in a clean greased basin, turning to grease all surfaces, cover with clean cloth and leave to rise in warm place until double in bulk (1-2 hours). Punch down dough and divide into four portions. Roll out each portion to a 10 x 4-in. (25 x 10-cm) rectangle. With back of knife make a lengthwise crease, slightly off-centre. Brush surface lightly with melted butter, fold along crease, wide side over narrow, and cut into five pieces. Place close together in greased baking tins, brush tops with butter and leave to rise 20 minutes. Bake in a moderately hot oven (400°F, 200°C, Gas Mark 6) for 15-20 minutes. Lay foil loosely over rolls if they brown too quickly.

20 rolls.

CRANBERRY	225 gm . 9 oz	plain flour
BREAD	75 gm . 3 oz	sugar
	1 tbsp	orange peel
	1¼ tsp . 1½ tsp	baking powder
	1 tsp	salt
	½ tsp	bicarbonate of soda
	165 ml . ⅓ pt	orange juice
	5 tsp . 2 tbsp	salad oil
	1	egg, beaten
	100 gm . 4 oz	chopped raw cranberries
	50 gm . 2 oz	chopped nuts

Combine flour, sugar, peel, baking powder, salt and bicarbonate of soda. Mix orange juice with oil and egg and stir into flour mixture. Add cranberries and nuts and pour into a greased loaf tin. Bake in a moderate oven (350°F, 180°C, Gas Mark 4) for about 40 minutes or until a knife inserted comes out clean.

Cranberry Muffins

Bake in greased patty tins, two-thirds full, 20 minutes.
About 18 muffins.

PUMPKIN PIE

		shortcrust pastry for single-crust pie
	2	eggs
450 gm .	1 lb	cooked mashed pumpkin (fresh or tinned)
140 gm .	5 oz	sugar
	½ tsp	salt
	1 tsp	cinnamon
	½ tsp	ginger
	¼ tsp	cloves
370 ml .	⅔ pt	evaporated milk

Prepare pastry and line a 9-in. (23-cm) pie plate.

Beat eggs and mix with pumpkin. Add sugar, salt and spices and blend well. Slowly add evaporated milk and stir until thoroughly mixed. Pour into the pastry shell and bake in a hot oven (450°F, 230°C, Gas Mark 8) for 10 minutes. Reduce heat (350°F, 180°C, Gas Mark 4) and bake until filling is set (about 30 minutes). Cool pie and serve with sweetened whipped cream.

MINCE PIE WITH HOT RUM SAUCE

		shortcrust pastry for double-crust pie
675 gm .	1½ lb	mincemeat
		Hot Rum Sauce

Prepare pastry and line 9-in. (23-cm) pie plate with half of it. Roll remaining dough into circle for top, cutting several short slits in it, or cut into strips and weave lattice top. Pour mincemeat into bottom crust, cover with top crust, and bake in a moderately hot oven (425°F, 220°C, Gas Mark 7) until crust is golden-brown (15-20 minutes). Serve warm with Hot Rum Sauce.

HOT RUM SAUCE

100 gm .	4 oz	sugar
1¾ tsp .	2 tsp	cornflour
250 ml .	½ pt	cold water
5 tsp .	2 tbsp	butter
2½ tbsp .	3 tbsp	rum
1¾ tsp .	2 tsp	lemon juice

Mix sugar with cornflour and add water gradually. Add butter, rum and lemon juice and cook, stirring, until thickened. Serve warm over Mince Pie.

TROY PUDDING

100 gm	4 oz	chopped suet
250 ml	½ pt	milk
190 ml	1½ gills	treacle
100 gm	4 oz	raisins
50 gm	2 oz	brown sugar
400 gm	1 lb	plain flour
1 tsp	1¼ tsp	bicarbonate of soda
	1 tsp	cloves
	½ tsp	salt

Combine suet, milk, treacle, raisins and brown sugar and mix well. Combine flour, soda, cloves and salt and mix with suet mixture. Turn into buttered basin, cover with foil and steam three hours. Serve hot with sweetened whipped cream.

Serves 8 — 10.

Southern Cooking

COTTON PLANTATIONS AND CREOLES:
NEGROES AND MOUNTAIN FOLK

Fourteen states make up the region known as The South. Four of the states, Delaware, Maryland, West Virginia and Kentucky, are considered Border States, while Alabama, Arkansas, Florida, Georgia, Louisiana, Mississippi, North Carolina, South Carolina, Tennessee and Virginia are often referred to as the Deep South. However, the South can be divided and redivided in many ways for its history is as varied as its geography. Swedish and Dutch came to Delaware, but most of the states along the Atlantic coast were originally settled by people from the British Isles. It was the Spanish and French who moved into the area along the Gulf of Mexico. After the Louisiana Purchase in 1803, all of the South belonged to the United States.

There is no composite picture of the South. One might envisage great plantations of tobacco or cotton with elegant white colonial mansions and magnolia trees. That is the South. Or one might think of tiny cabins in the remote areas of the Blue Ridge Mountains, the Great Smokies, or the Ozarks. That also is the South. So, too, are the rich blue grasses and thoroughbred racehorses of Kentucky, the big-game fishing for tarpon and sailfish off the Florida coast, the alligators and cypress trees of the bayous, and the fragrant jasmine and bougainvillea which grow wild in the warm, humid climate.

The city of New Orleans has many facets. The customs of the Creoles (descendants of early French and Spanish settlers) have been adopted also by people who came later from the northern states. New Orleans has a large Negro population and the city is noted as the birthplace of jazz. The old French Quarter is elegant wrought-iron balconies and flower-filled patios. Mardi Gras is a festival of parades and parties and fancy dress balls which lasts from Twelfth Night to Shrove Tuesday. Above all, New Orleans is noted for its fine Creole cuisine.

Other parts of the South are also known for excellent food. A long coastline on both the Atlantic Ocean and the Gulf of Mexico provides an abundance of shellfish for such dishes as Maryland Crab Cakes and Oysters Rockefeller. Peanuts from Alabama, peaches from Georgia, citrus fruits from Florida, and chicken and corn and blackeyed peas from all over; Southern cooking includes them all.

SMOTHERED PORK CHOPS

	4 large	pork chops
	¼ tsp	sage
	¼ tsp	thyme
	1 tsp	salt
	⅛ tsp	pepper
	1 large	onion, sliced
125 ml .	1 gill	water
2½ tsp .	1 tbsp	cornflour
5 tsp .	2 tbsp	cold water
125 ml .	1 gill	sour cream

Sprinkle pork chops with sage, thyme, salt and pepper. Fry slowly until brown on both sides. Pour off excess fat. Add onion and 1 gill water and simmer, covered, 40 minutes. Remove chops to a warm platter. Mix cornflour with cold water and stir into the liquid in the pan. Cook, stirring, until thickened. Add sour cream and heat, but do not boil. Spoon sauce over chops.
Serves 4.

FRIED CHICKEN

1¼ kg .	2½ lb	frying chicken, cut into joints
50 gm .	2 oz	plain flour
	2 tsp	salt
	½ tsp	pepper
		fat or oil for frying

Mix flour, salt and pepper and coat chicken with mixture. Heat fat or oil in large frying pan. It should be about ⅛ in. (3 mm) deep. Add chicken pieces and fry until browned on both sides. Pour off excess fat, cover frying pan, and cook over low heat 30 minutes. Remove cover and raise heat for 5 minutes to crisp chicken. Remove to ovenproof platter or dish and place in very low oven 30 minutes.

Creamy Chicken Gravy

Add 3 tablespoons flour to 3 tablespoons fat in frying pan and blend smoothly. Pour in ½ pt (275 ml) water and 1 gill (140 ml) milk and cook, stirring, until thickened. Add salt and pepper to taste.

CHICKEN GUMBO

1 l.	1 qt	chicken broth
	2	beef stock cubes
	1 large	onion, chopped
	3	tomatoes, peeled and chopped
	⅛ tsp	cayenne pepper
	¼ tsp	thyme
100 gm.	4 oz	boneless cooked chicken, finely diced
		salt
50 gm.	2 oz	white rice

Combine broth, beef cubes, onion, tomatoes, cayenne and thyme and bring to boil. Simmer, covered, for one hour, stirring occasionally. Add salt to taste. Add rice and continue cooking for 30 minutes. Add diced chicken and cook 10 minutes, uncovered.

Serves 4.

COUNTRY CAPTAIN

250 gm.	10 oz	cooked boneless chicken
2½ tbsp.	3 tbsp	butter
	2	onions, chopped
	½	green pepper, chopped
	1 clove	garlic, crushed
5 tsp.	2 tbsp	curry powder
1¼ tsp.	1½ tsp	salt
	¼ tsp	pepper
3½ tbsp.	4 tbsp	flour
500 ml.	1 pt	chicken broth
125 ml.	1 gill	cream or evaporated milk
50 gm.	2 oz	raisins
	1	cooking apple, diced
		cooked white rice
	2	spring onions, chopped
25 gm.	1 oz	slivered almonds
		chutney

Melt butter and add onion, green pepper, garlic, curry, salt and pepper. Cook gently until tender. Stir in flour. Gradually add broth and cream and cook, stirring, until thickened. Add chicken, apple and raisins, and continue cooking and stirring until heated. Serve over cooked rice with almonds and onions sprinkled on top. Serve chutney as an accompaniment.

Serves 4 — 6.

BRUNSWICK STEW

300 gm .	12 oz	boneless cooked chicken, cubed
50 gm .	2 oz	bacon, chopped
	1	onion, peeled and quartered
400 gm .	1 lb	tomatoes, peeled and chopped
	2 sticks	celery, chopped
200 gm .	8 oz	butter beans or broad beans
	2 medium	potatoes, diced
1 l. .	1 qt	chicken broth
2½ tsp .	1 tbsp	sugar
	½	bay leaf
	2 tbsp	chopped parsley
	dash	cayenne pepper
	½ tsp	black pepper
		salt to taste
200 gm .	8 oz	frozen sweet corn

Fry bacon until crisp. Combine onion, tomatoes, celery, beans and potatoes with broth and seasonings and bacon in large saucepan. Simmer until vegetables are tender. Stir frequently. Add sweet corn and chicken and continue cooking for 15 minutes.

Serves 6 — 8.

Turkey Brunswick Stew

Substitute cooked turkey for chicken in above recipe.

SHRIMP CREOLE

2½ tbsp .	3 tbsp	butter
	1	onion, finely chopped
	1	green pepper, chopped
	1 stick	celery, chopped
	1 clove	garlic, crushed
2½ tsp .	1 tbsp	plain flour
	1 tsp	salt
	⅛ tsp	cayenne pepper
	1 tsp	chilli powder
1¾ tsp .	2 tsp	Worcestershire sauce
200 gm .	8 oz	tinned tomato purée
400 gm .	1 lb	tinned tomatoes
400 gm .	1 lb	cooked shelled shrimps

Melt butter and fry onion, green pepper, celery and garlic until tender. Stir in flour, salt, cayenne, chilli powder and Worcestershire sauce, tomato purée and tomatoes. Simmer gently, stirring occasionally, for one hour. Add shrimps and cook 5 minutes. Serve with hot cooked rice.

Serves 6.

DEVILLED CRAB	75 gm . 3 oz	butter
MARYLAND	1	green pepper, finely chopped
	½	onion, minced
	2½ tbsp . 3 tbsp	plain flour
	2½ tsp . 3 tsp	mustard powder
	¾ tsp	salt
	190 ml . 1½ gills	milk
	2½ tbsp . 3 tbsp	brandy
	25 gm . 1 oz	fine dry breadcrumbs
	600 gm . 1½ lb	crab meat

Fry green pepper and onion in 3 tablespoons of the butter until tender. Stir in flour, mustard and salt. Add milk gradually and stir in brandy. Cook, stirring, over low heat until thickened. Gently stir in crab and spoon into an ovenproof dish. Sprinkle with breadcrumbs and dot with remaining butter. Bake in a moderate oven (375° F, 190° C, Gas Mark 5) for 20 minutes or until browned.

Serves 4 — 6.

JAMBOLAYA	5 tsp . 2 tbsp	butter or margarine
	100 gm . 4 oz	cooked diced ham
	1	onion, chopped
	1 clove	garlic, crushed
	250 ml . ½ pt	water
	400 gm . 1 lb	tinned tomatoes
	2	beef stock cubes
	1 tbsp	chopped parsley
	1	bay leaf
	¼ tsp	thyme
	⅛ tsp	cayenne pepper
	⅛ tsp	black pepper
	150 gm . 6 oz	white rice
	300 gm . 12 oz	cooked shelled shrimp
	1	green pepper, cut into strips

Melt butter and fry ham, onion and garlic until tender. Add remaining ingredients except shrimp and green pepper and mix well. Simmer, covered, until rice is tender, stirring occasionally (about 20 minutes). Remove bay leaf. Stir in shrimp and green pepper and cook 5 minutes.

Serves 6.

OYSTERS ROCKEFELLER

	2 dozen	oysters in shells
	½ small	onion, minced
	3 tbsp	finely chopped parsley
	½ stick	celery, finely chopped
50 gm .	2 oz	butter or margarine
50 gm .	2 oz	fresh raw spinach, finely chopped
50 gm .	2 oz	fine dry breadcrumbs
	¼ tsp	salt
	4 tbsp	butter
		paprika

Prise open shells with sharp knife, remove oysters and drain them. Wash deep halves of shells and place an oyster on each. Fry onion, parsley and celery in butter until tender. Add spinach, breadcrumbs and salt and cook, stirring, 1 minute. Place a spoonful of spinach mixture on each oyster, top with ½ teaspoon of butter and sprinkle lightly with paprika. Bake in a hot oven (450° F, 230° C, Gas Mark 8) for 10 minutes or until browned. Serve in shells as a first course.

MARYLAND CRAB CAKES

450 gm .	1 lb	crab meat
	1 tsp	salt
	½ tsp	pepper
	1 tsp	mustard powder
	2 tsp	Worcestershire sauce
	1 tbsp	mayonnaise
	1 tbsp	chopped parsley
	1	egg yolk
	4 tbsp	fine dry breadcrumbs
	3 tbsp	melted butter
		additional breadcrumbs for coating
		butter or fat for frying

Combine crab, salt, pepper, mustard, Worcestershire sauce, mayonnaise, parsley, egg yolk, breadcrumbs and melted butter and mix well. Shape into six cakes and coat with crumbs. Fry in butter or fat over medium heat until golden-brown on both sides.

Serves 6.

PEANUT SOUP

50 gm	2 oz	butter or margarine
	¼	onion, minced
	2 tbsp	plain flour
100 gm	4 oz	peanut butter
500 ml	1 pt	chicken broth
	'1 tsp	salt
	¼ tsp	pepper
250 ml	½ pt	milk
125 ml	1 gill	cream or evaporated milk

Fry onion in butter until tender. Stir in flour. Add peanut butter, broth, salt and pepper, and cook, stirring, until thickened. Gradually stir in milk and cream and continue cooking, stirring, until heated.
Serves 6 — 8.

HOPPIN' JOHN

100 gm	4 oz	streaky bacon, diced
	½	onion, chopped
1 l.	1 qt	water
100 gm	4 oz	white rice
400 gm	1 lb	tinned blackeyed peas
1¾ tsp	2 tsp	salt

Fry bacon and onion together until tender. In a large saucepan place water, rice, blackeyed peas (including liquid), salt and bacon-onion mixture (including fat). Simmer 10 minutes. Drain and serve.
Serves 6.

SOUTHERN CORN BREAD

125 gm	5 oz	plain flour
125 gm	5 oz	yellow cornmeal
2½ tbsp	3 tbsp	sugar
4½ tsp	5 tsp	baking powder
	¼ tsp	salt
	1	egg, beaten
250 ml	½ pt	milk
2 tbsp	2½ tbsp	cooking oil

Sieve dry ingredients together. Combine egg, milk and oil and mix well with flour mixture. Pour into greased 9-in. (23-cm) square baking tin and bake in a moderately hot oven (425°F, 220°C, Gas Mark 7) for 20-25 minutes. Cut into squares and serve warm.

CREOLE SAUCE

	2	onions, chopped
	1	green pepper, chopped
	2 tsp	salt
	¼ tsp	pepper
	1 clove	garlic, crushed
	dash	cayenne pepper
	1	bay leaf
550 ml .	1 pt	tomato juice
	4 tbsp	butter
	3 tbsp	plain flour

Combine all ingredients except butter and flour in saucepan. Simmer 30 minutes, stirring occasionally. Strain. Blend butter and flour together and add to mixture. Cook, stirring, until thickened. Serve with meat.

PEANUT BUTTER BREAD

100 gm .	4 oz	peanut butter
5 tsp .	2 tbsp	salad oil
125 gm .	5 oz	sugar
	1	egg
280 ml .	½ pt +2 tbsp	milk
200 gm .	8 oz	plain flour
2½ tsp .	3 tsp	baking powder
	¼ tsp	salt

Cream peanut butter, oil and sugar together. Beat in egg, add milk and mix well. Sieve flour, baking powder and salt together and stir into first mixture. Pour into buttered loaf tin and bake in a moderate oven (350° F, 180°C, Gas Mark 4) for one hour or until inserted knife comes out clean.

Orange-Peanut Butter Bread

Use orange juice in place of milk in above recipe.

HUSH PUPPIES

125 gm .	5 oz	yellow cornmeal
65 gm .	2½ oz	plain flour
1¾ tsp .	2 tsp	baking powder
	1 tsp	salt
	1 small	onion, minced
	1	egg, beaten
65 ml .	½ gill	milk
5 tsp .	2 tbsp	water

Sieve cornmeal, flour, baking powder and salt together. Add onion, egg, milk and water and mix well. Heat fat in frying pan to ¼ in. (6 mm) depth. Shape mixture into small patties and fry in hot fat until golden and crisp on both sides. Drain on paper towels. Serve with fried fish.

About 18 patties.

SPOON BREAD

550ml .	1 pt	milk
	1 tbsp	butter
115 gm .	4 oz	yellow cornmeal
	1 tsp	salt
	2	eggs, separated

Heat milk with butter. Add cornmeal and salt and cook in top of double saucepan until thick. Cool slightly. Beat egg yolks and combine with cornmeal mixture. Beat egg whites until stiff and fold in. Pour into greased ovenproof dish and bake in a moderate oven (375° F, 190° C, Gas Mark 5) until firm (about 40 minutes). Serve warm with butter, in place of potatoes.

Serves 4 — 6.

NEW ORLEANS CHERRIES JUBILEE

450 gm .	1 lb	tinned sweet black cherries (stoned)
	2 tsp	lemon juice
	2 tbsp	orange juice
	1 tbsp	cornflour
140 ml .	1 gill	brandy
		vanilla ice cream

Combine liquid from cherries with lemon juice, orange juice and cornflour in a chafing dish. Cook over low heat, stirring, until thickened. Add cherries and continue cooking and stirring until mixture is bubbly. Turn off flame, pour brandy over cherries and ignite. Serve hot over vanilla ice cream.

Serves 4 — 6.

SOUTHERN BANANA PUDDING

	2	eggs
15 gm .	½ oz	cornflour
60 gm .	2 oz	sugar
600 ml .	1 pt	milk
	1 tsp	vanilla essence
90 gm .	3 oz	soft sweet biscuits, crumbled
	4	bananas, sliced

37

Mix eggs, cornflour and sugar. Add milk gradually. Cook, stirring, over low heat until thickened. Cool slightly and stir in vanilla. Spread half of biscuit crumbs in a dish and top with half of the bananas. Repeat layers. Pour the custard over. Chill and top with whipped cream.

Serves 6.

OZARK PIE

100 gm .	4 oz	plain flour
200 gm .	8 oz	sugar
2 tsp .	2¼ tsp	baking powder
	1 tsp	salt
500 gm .	1¼ lb	apples, peeled, cored and chopped
50 gm .	2 oz	chopped nuts
	2	eggs, beaten
	1 tsp	vanilla essence

Combine flour, sugar, baking powder and salt. Add chopped apple and nuts. Beat in eggs and vanilla. Pour into greased 9-in (23-cm) sandwich tin and bake in a moderate oven (375°F, 190°C, Gas Mark 5) for 40-45 minutes. Serve warm with whipped cream.

Serves 6.

LADY BALTIMORE CAKE

150 gm .	6 oz	butter
250 gm .	10 oz	sugar
	¾ tsp	vanilla essence
225 gm .	9 oz	plain flour
2½ tsp .	3 tsp	baking powder
	¼ tsp	salt
165 ml .	⅓ pt	milk
	4	egg whites
		Lady Baltimore Filling and Frosting

Cream butter with sugar thoroughly. Beat in vanilla essence. Sieve flour with baking powder and salt and add to creamed mixture alternately with milk. Beat egg whites until stiff and fold into mixture. Spread mixture in three buttered and floured 8-in. (20-cm) sandwich tins and bake in a moderate oven (350°F, 180°C, Gas Mark 4) until done (about 40 minutes). Put layers together with Lady Baltimore Filling and ice top and sides with Lady Baltimore Frosting.

Lady Baltimore	275 ml . ½ pt	light corn syrup
Filling and Frosting	2	egg whites
	pinch	salt
	50 gm . 2 oz	raisins
	50 gm . 2 oz	chopped nuts

Heat syrup to boiling. Set aside. Beat egg whites and salt until stiff. Continue beating while pouring hot syrup slowly into egg whites. Divide mixture into two equal parts. To one part add raisins and nuts and use as Filling for Lady Baltimore Cake. Use remainder to ice top and sides of cake.

GEORGIA PEACH COBBLER

	75 gm . 3 oz	sugar
	2½ tsp . 1 tbsp	cornflour
	600 gm . 1½ lb	fresh peaches
	¼ tsp	cinnamon
	1 tsp	lemon juice
	100 gm . 4 oz	plain flour
	5 tsp . 2 tbsp	sugar
	1¼ tsp . 1½ tsp	baking powder
	¼ tsp	salt
	3 tbsp	melted butter
	125 ml . 1 gill	milk

Peel, stone and slice peaches. Add sugar, cornflour, cinnamon and lemon juice and mix well. Cook and stir over medium heat until thickened and bubbly. Pour into ovenproof dish. Mix flour, sugar, baking powder and salt. Combine melted butter and milk and add to flour mixture. Spoon dough on to hot fruit and bake in a moderately hot oven (400°F, 200°C, Gas Mark 6) until golden-brown (25-30 minutes).

Serves 6.

PECAN PIE

		shortcrust pastry for single-crust pie
	3½ tbsp . 4 tbsp	butter
	150 gm . 6 oz	brown sugar
	dash	salt
	190 ml . 1½ gills	dark corn syrup
	3	eggs, beaten
	1 tsp	vanilla essence
	100 gm . 4 oz	pecan or walnut halves

Prepare pastry and line 9-in. (23-cm) pie plate.

Cream butter with sugar and salt. Stir in syrup, beaten eggs and vanilla. Spread nuts evenly in pastry and pour mixture over them. Bake in a hot oven (450°F, 230°C, Gas Mark 8) 10 minutes, reduce heat (350°F, 180°C, Gas Mark 4) and bake 30 minutes or until set.

PEANUT BUTTER PIE

		shortcrust pastry for single-crust pie, baked
2½ tbsp	3 tbsp	cornflour
100 gm	4 oz	sugar
	1	egg
500 ml	1 pt	cold milk
125 gm	5 oz	peanut butter
		sweetened whipped cream

Prepare and bake pastry crust in 9-in. (23-cm) pie plate. Cool.

Mix cornflour, sugar and egg and gradually stir in milk. Add peanut butter and cook over low heat, stirring, until peanut butter has melted and mixture is thick and smooth. Pour into baked crust and chill. Serve topped with whipped cream.

Chocolate Peanut Butter Pie

Add 3 tablespoons cocoa to cornflour in above recipe.

PEANUT BUTTER COOKIES

100 gm	4 oz	butter or margarine
125 gm	5 oz	peanut butter
75 gm	3 oz	granulated sugar
100 gm	4 oz	brown sugar
	1	egg
	½ tsp	vanilla essence
100 gm	4 oz	plain flour
	½ tsp	salt
	½ tsp	bicarbonate of soda

Cream butter and peanut butter together. Add sugars and beat well. Beat in egg and vanilla. Sieve together flour, salt and soda and stir into mixture. Drop by heaped teaspoonfuls onto baking sheet and press flat with fork, leaving marks of tines. Bake in a moderate oven (350° F, 180° C, Gas Mark 4) until firm (about 10 minutes).

4-5 dozen cookies.

PEANUT BUTTER ICING

75 gm	3 oz	peanut butter
3½ tbsp	4 tbsp	boiling water
350 gm	14 oz	icing sugar

Pour boiling water over peanut butter and mix well. Gradually beat in sugar. Use as icing for cakes.

Chocolate Peanut Butter Icing

Add 1 oz (25 gm) cocoa to sugar in above recipe.

KEY LIME PIE

	shortcrust pastry for single-crust pie
1 tbsp	unflavoured gelatine
70 ml . ½ gill	boiling water
3	egg yolks
275 ml . ½ pt	sweet condensed milk
140 ml . 1 gill	lime juice
few drops	green food colouring
3	egg whites
5 tbsp	sugar

Prepare pastry and bake in a 9-in. (23-cm) pie plate. Cool.

Sprinkle gelatine on boiling water and stir to dissolve. Chill until syrupy but not set. Beat egg yolks, add condensed milk, lime juice and food colour and gelatine mixture. Mix well and pour into cooled baked crust. Beat egg whites until stiff. Add sugar, one tablespoon at a time, beating well after each addition. Spread over filling. Place under hot grill until pale gold (3-5 minutes).

PEACH CONSERVE

1 kg . 2½ lb	fresh peaches
2	oranges
2 tbsp	lemon juice
75 gm . 3 oz	raisins
850 gm . 2 lb	sugar
50 gm . 2 oz	chopped nuts

Drop peaches into boiling water, a few at a time, until skins split. Plunge into cold water. Slip off skins. Stone and chop peaches. Peel oranges thinly and cut peel into small pieces. Discard white pith and seeds and chop oranges. Combine peaches, oranges, peel, lemon juice, raisins and sugar in a large saucepan and cook, stirring occasionally, until very thick (1-1½ hours). Add nuts. Pour into hot sterilized jars and seal.

MINT JULEP

1 tsp	sugar
2 tsp	water
6	mint leaves
	crushed ice
3 tbsp	bourbon whiskey

Mix sugar, water and mint leaves in a chilled glass. Fill with crushed ice and pour whiskey over. Stir until glass is frosty on outside.

CAFÉ BRÛLOT

8 lumps	sugar
140 ml . 1 gill	Cognac brandy
2 sticks	cinnamon
12	whole cloves
1 slice	lemon
275 ml . 1 pt	strong black coffee

Combine all ingredients except coffee in a chafing dish and stir until hot. Ignite and allow to burn for 30 seconds. Slowly add hot coffee and stir. Serve in demitasse cups.

COFFEE PUNCH

500 ml . 1 pt	thick cream
1¾ tsp . 2 tsp	vanilla essence
1 l . 2 pt	vanilla ice cream
2 l . 2 qt	cold strong black coffee

Stir cream, vanilla and ice cream together until blended. Slowly stir in coffee and mix well. Serve in a punchbowl.
   Serves 20.

Brandied Coffee Punch

Add 1 pt (500 ml) brandy to above recipe.

Texas and the Southwest

THE MEXICAN INFLUENCE

Only four states, Arizona, New Mexico, Oklahoma and Texas, make up the Southwest region, but Texas is so large that together these states form an area more than eight times the size of New England. There is room for bigness. For the giant Saguara cactus which grows fifty feet high, for the thousands of great oil derricks which rise above the horizon, for endless miles of plains and desert, for cattle ranches which cover hundreds of thousands of acres each, room even for the Grand Canyon.

The Southwest has a unique beauty. In the Painted Desert of Arizona, pinnacles and buttes catch the rays of the setting sun, reflecting yellow and azure, crimson and amethyst. Cactus blooms in the dry warmth of the desert and sagebrush scents the air. Forests grow over the slopes of the Rocky Mountains which extend into New Mexico, and palm trees grow along the Gulf Coast beaches of Texas.

History has been trodden into the trails of the Southwest. The oldest road in the United States, El Camino Real, was built by the Spaniards in the sixteenth century. It extends from Santa Fé in New Mexico to Mexico City, two thousand miles to the south. In the early nineteenth century covered wagons began to roll along the Sante Fé Trail, from Missouri to New Mexico, bringing thousands of Anglo-Americans into the region. Thousands of cattle were driven along the Chisholm Trail from Texas to Kansas, from where they could be shipped by rail to the stockyards and packing houses of the Midwest.

The culture of Southwestern United States is a blend of Spanish, Indian and Anglo-American. The Spanish began to explore the area in the early sixteenth century, eventually establishing missions and colonies. The Spanish heritage is reflected in the names of many cities: El Paso, Santa Fé, Casa Grande, and San Antonio. Much of the Southwest was at one time part of Mexico and many people have moved into the area from Mexico, bringing with them a culture which is partly Spanish and partly Indian. There are many Indians in the Southwestern states, some of them descendants of the early Pueblo Indians, or cliff-dwellers. In the nineteenth century, large numbers of settlers arrived from eastern states, from Canada, Great Britain, and from the European continent. They built up great herds of cattle and sheep, planted cotton and rice and citrus groves. This blending of cultures is evident in the variety of festivals held each year in the Southwest: Indian Pow-wows and Fire Dances, Spanish Fiestas and Carnivals, Livestock shows, Rodeos and Citrus Festivals.

Irrigation and the warm climate make possible the production of melons, grapefruit, dates, onions, lettuce, and pecans. Tomatoes, peppers, and sweet potatoes are important foods also, and great red garlands of chilli peppers can be seen hanging to dry in the villages at harvest time. However, as in other parts of the North American continent, corn and beans are staple foods. Red or pink beans, known as frijoles, are cooked for many hours, and often cooked a second time with cheese, when they become frijoles refritos, or refried beans. The corn is ground into meal and made into flat cakes called tortillas. These are folded over fillings of meat, cheese, or beans, sometimes baked (enchiladas) or fried (tacos), and the seasonings are as hot as the desert sands.

TEXAS	125 ml . 1 gill	boiling water
BARBECUED	65 ml . ½ gill	vinegar
BEEF	3½ tbsp . 4 tbsp	lemon juice
	250 ml . ½ pt	dry red wine
	½	onion, chopped
	4 tsp . 1½ tbsp	Worcestershire sauce
	¼ tsp	cayenne pepper
	1¾ tsp . 2 tsp	salt
	100 gm . 4 oz	cooking oil
	1¼ kg . 3 lb	lean stewing steak, cut into serving-size pieces

Combine all ingredients except beef and boil five minutes. Lay steak in large shallow dish and pour marinade over it. Cover and refrigerate 24 hours, turning meat occasionally. Cook steaks over a barbecue fire, basting frequently with marinade, until well done on both sides. *Or* cook meat under a hot grill, basting frequently.

Serves 6 — 8.

TEXAS CHILLI	900 gm . 2 lb	stewing beef, cut into small cubes
	1 tbsp	cooking fat or oil
	1	onion, chopped
	2 cloves	garlic, crushed
	2-3 tbsp	chilli powder
	3 tbsp	plain flour
	550 ml . 1 pt	water
	2 tsp	salt
	¼ tsp	pepper

Heat oil and brown beef with onion and garlic. Sprinkle chilli powder and flour over meat and onion and stir until blended. Add water, salt and pepper and stir until mixture begins to boil. Cover pan and simmer gently for 2 hours, or until meat is very tender.

Chilli con Frijoles

Add 1pt (550 ml) cooked or tinned red beans or haricot beans to cooked Chilli and continue cooking 15 minutes.

FRIJOLES

450 gm .	1 lb	dry red beans or pink pinto beans
	1 large	onion, chopped
	1 tbsp	olive oil or salad oil
		salt

Soak beans overnight in cold water to cover. Drain and cover with fresh water. Add onion, oil and simmer until tender (about 2 hours), stirring occasionally and adding more water if necessary. Drain. Add salt to taste.

Frijoles Refritos

		Frijoles
	¼ tsp	salt
	⅛ tsp	cayenne pepper
25 gm .	1 oz	bacon drippings

Prepare Frijoles and mash with salt and cayenne pepper. Fry in the bacon drippings until brown.
Serves 6 — 8.

TAMALE PIE

500 ml .	1 pt	water
	1 tsp	salt
250 ml .	½ pt	milk
125 gm .	5 oz	yellow cornmeal
25 gm .	1 oz	butter or margarine
	1 small	onion, chopped
	1 small	green pepper, chopped
	1 clove	garlic, crushed
400 gm .	1 lb	minced raw beef
5 tsp .	2 tbsp	plain flour
250 ml .	½ pt	tomato purée

400 gm .	1 lb	tinned tomatoes
	8	black olives, stoned and chopped
1¾ tsp .	2 tsp	chilli powder
	¼ tsp	pepper
	1 tsp	salt
2½ tsp .	1 tbsp	butter
3½ tbsp .	4 tbsp	milk
50 gm .	2 oz	grated Cheddar cheese

Mix water, salt, milk and cornmeal in a saucepan. Cook over low heat, stirring, until mixture begins to bubble. Continue cooking, stirring frequently, for 15 minutes. Fry onion, green pepper and garlic in butter until limp. Add beef and continue cooking until meat is no longer pink. Stir in flour, tomato pureé, tomatoes, olives, chilli powder, pepper and salt and cook, stirring frequently, 15 minutes. Spread two-thirds of cornmeal mixture over bottom of ovenproof dish, pushing mixture up the sides. Pour in meat mixture. Stir butter, milk and cheese into remaining cornmeal mixture and spread over top of meat. Bake in a moderate oven (350° F, 180° C, Gas Mark 4) for 30 minutes.

Serves 6.

ENCHILADA CASSEROLE

6	Corn Tortillas, frozen or tinned
	or
6	Cornmeal Pancakes (recipe follows)
	Enchilada Filling
	grated Cheddar cheese

Fry Tortillas gently in lightly greased frying pan just until softened, or prepare Cornmeal Pancakes. Prepare Enchilada Filling (recipes following). Layer Filling and tortillas in ovenproof dish, with Filling at bottom and on top. Sprinkle with grated cheese and bake in a moderate oven (350° F, 180° C, Gas Mark 4) for 30 minutes.

Serves 4.

CORNMEAL PANCAKES

140 gm .	5 oz	yellow cornmeal
	4 tbsp	plain flour
	1 tsp	baking powder
	½ tsp	salt
	1	egg
	5 tbsp	milk
140 ml .	1 gill	water
	3 tbsp	salad oil

Mix cornmeal, flour, baking powder and salt together. Beat egg, add milk, water and oil and mix well. Blend in dry ingredients. Spoon onto hot griddle or frying pan, lightly greased, using 6 tablespoons for each cake. (Pancakes should be about 6 in., or 15 cm, in diameter.) Cook on both sides. Stack on a plate with paper towels between.

6 pancakes.

ENCHILADA FILLING NO. 1	450 gm . 1 lb	stewing steak, finely chopped
	1	onion, chopped
	1 clove	garlic, crushed
	2 tbsp	cooking oil
	1 tbsp	plain flour
	½ tsp	salt
	1 tbsp	chilli powder
	140 ml . 1 gill	water
	140 ml . 1 gill	tomato purée

Cook meat, onion and garlic together in hot oil until browned. Stir in flour, salt and chilli powder. Add water and tomato purée gradually and cook until thick. Simmer, covered, stirring frequently, until meat is very tender.

ENCHILADA FILLING NO. 2	450 gm . 1 lb	minced raw beef
	1	onion, chopped
	1 clove	garlic, crushed
	1 tsp	salt
	¼ tsp	pepper
	2 tbsp	chilli powder
	4 tbsp	plain flour
	450 gm . 1 lb	tinned tomato purée
	140 ml . 1 gill	water

Stir beef, onion and garlic together over medium heat until browned. Stir in salt, pepper, chilli powder and flour. Add tomato purée and water and cook, stirring, until thickened. Simmer gently, stirring frequently, 10 minutes.

SPANISH OMELETTE	2 tbsp	salad oil
	1	onion, chopped
	1 clove	garlic, crushed
	½ tsp	salt
	½ tsp	oregano
	¼ tsp	ginger

	1 tbsp	chilli powder
340 gm .	12 oz	tomatoes, peeled and chopped
	6	eggs
	½ tsp	salt
	⅛ tsp	pepper
	2 tbsp	butter

Fry onion and garlic in oil until tender. Add salt, oregano, ginger, chilli powder and tomatoes and simmer 15 minutes, stirring occasionally. Beat eggs with salt and pepper. Heat butter in omelette pan or frying pan and add eggs. Cook over medium heat without stirring. Lift edges occasionally and tilt pan so mixture will run underneath. When eggs are set, slide omelette onto warm platter. Spoon sauce over and fold in half.

Serves 2 — 3.

EGGS RANCHEROS

	4 tbsp	butter
	2 cloves	garlic, crushed
	1	onion, chopped very fine
	2 tbsp	plain flour
	4	tomatoes, peeled and finely chopped
	3 tsp	chilli powder
	½ tsp	marjoram
	½ tsp	thyme
	1 tsp	salt
	8	fried eggs

Fry garlic and onion in butter until tender. Stir in flour. Add tomatoes, chilli, marjoram, thyme and salt and cook on low heat, stirring frequently, 20 minutes. Serve sauce over fried eggs.

SPANISH RICE

50 gm .	2 oz	butter
	½	green pepper, chopped
	1	onion, chopped
150 gm .	6 oz	uncooked white rice
	½ tsp	salt
	¼ tsp	pepper
625 ml .	1¼ pt	tomato juice

In melted butter, fry green pepper, onion and rice 10 minutes. Add salt, pepper and tomato juice and simmer, covered, 20 minutes or until rice is tender.

Serves 4 — 6.

BEAN DIP

450 gm .	1 lb	tinned kidney beans, undrained
	2 tbsp	minced onion
	1 tbsp	chilli powder
25 gm .	1 oz	Cheddar cheese, grated

Heat beans with onion and chilli and simmer, covered, 20 minutes. Mash thoroughly. Add cheese and stir until melted. Serve hot or cold as a dip for crackers or potato crisps.

GUACAMOLE

3	avocadoes, peeled and chopped
1	tomato, peeled and chopped
1 small	onion, peeled and finely chopped
1 tsp	salt
¼ tsp	pepper
dash	cayenne pepper
2 tsp	vinegar
1 tsp	mayonnaise

Combine all ingredients and beat until smooth (or use liquidizer). Serve as a dip for raw vegetables or crackers, or as a salad dressing for lettuce and tomatoes.

VERY HOT SAUCE

2	tomatoes, peeled and chopped
3 tbsp	chilli powder
1	onion, minced
4 tbsp	water

Combine all ingredients in a small saucepan and simmer 30 minutes, stirring frequently. Serve as a condiment.

MARGARITA COCKTAIL

4 tbsp	tequila
2 tbsp	Cointreau or Triple Sec liqueur
½	fresh lime
	ice cubes
	salt

Mix tequila, Cointreau, lime juice and ice cubes. Spread salt on a small plate. Rub rim of cocktail glass with the lime and twirl in the salt. Strain the cocktail into the glass.

The Western Frontier

THE OLD WEST
(cowboys, goldmines, chuckwagons and sourdough)
THE NEW WEST
(Golden Gate Bridge and Alaskan pipeline)

The West was an unknown region to early American settlers along the Atlantic coast, but the less trepid gradually moved the frontier across the Appalachian Mountains. Spanish and English explorers discovered the continent's west coast, and Spanish missions were established in California in the eighteenth century. However, the vast area in between was known only to Indians and a few trappers and mountain men until the Lewis and Clark Expedition in 1804. By the middle of the nineteenth century, the covered wagons had begun to cross the prairies and the Rocky Mountains into Oregon. The discovery of gold in California in 1849 was a magnet which brought thousands, the same magnet which drew thousands more to Alaska at the end of the century. Brigham Young led his Mormon followers into Utah. Land brought them too, and there were fortunes to be made in new cities like San Francisco where prospectors came to spend their gold when they struck it rich, or to find work when they failed.

Whether they came for gold or land, to work as cowboys on the sprawling cattle ranches, or as pioneering families seeking a new life in the coastal valleys, they shared incredible hardships. Prairie summers were hot and mountain winters were cold, Indians were hostile, and outlaws roamed the area.

Food was scarce and simple. Sacks of flour, beans and coffee; salt pork; molasses; and a jar of sourdough; these were the basics for covered wagon and cattle-ranch chuckwagon alike. The sourdough starter was precious, and stories were told of prospectors who slept with their sourdough on cold nights to keep the yeast alive. Part of the sourdough went into the pancakes or bread in the morning, and flour and water were added to the remainder. The yeast grew and the process could be repeated indefinitely. San Francisco is still famous for its sourdough bread, and some cooks claim their starter goes back to Gold Rush days.

The rapid growth of the West brought a need for a railway. One line was begun on the west coast and another in the east. The two came together in Utah in 1869, joined by the Golden Spike which created a coast-to-coast railroad. The trains carried cattle to eastern markets and manufactured goods to the West. They carried people also, and the West grew rapidly as thousands came, from Europe as well as from the Atlantic coast. Chinese had come to work on the railway, and they stayed to open shops and laundries and restaurants. San Francisco's Chinatown became one of the largest Chinese communities outside China.

Today in the West, the peaks of the Rocky Mountains, Sierra Nevadas and Cascades still rise above 10,000 feet, but skiers and snowmobiles glide over the snowy slopes. The forests of the Northwest still seem endless, but trucks carry giant logs down mountain highways to sawmills in the valleys. Huge dams straddle the great rivers, providing electricity, and water for irrigation. Deserts grow golden with wheat, and cattle and sheep graze where once there were thousands of buffaloes. But the buffalo herds are increasing, and Western shoppers sometimes find buffalo meat in the supermarkets. Rivers and lakes still teem with trout for sport fishermen, but fleets of trawlers carry tuna and salmon to coastal canneries. Deer and elk and bears are still numerous and their meat is not strange to Western dinner tables, but neither are oranges and avocadoes from California, potatoes from Idaho, apples from Washington's Yakima Valley, or nuts and berries from orchards and farms of the Willamette Valley in Oregon. There is wine from Napa and Sonoma, and oysters from Puget Sound.

The West is still wide open spaces where wild horses and cattle outnumber people, but it is also people. People who grow things, who cut trees or work in sawmills, or in factories where jumbo jets are manufactured. People who live on farms or in small towns or in great cities like San Francisco, Seattle, Salt Lake City, Portland, Los Angeles, Denver, and Anchorage. Their customs and festivals reflect their national origins and their way of life: Old Spanish Days Fiesta and Chinese New Year; Shakespearean Festival and Indian Sun Dances; Whale Feast and Sled Dog Derby; Rodeo and Roundup; Timber Carnival and Gold Rush Festival; Oktoberfest and Scandinavian Fair; Winter Carnival and White Water Parade. Festivals mean food, and the American West has an abundance and variety of food. The Western cook must be versatile.

PAN-FRIED TROUT	900 gm . 2 lb	trout, cleaned and pan-ready
		flour, salt, pepper
		cooking fat or oil or
		bacon drippings

Sprinkle trout lightly with salt and pepper inside and out. Coat well with flour. Heat fat in large frying pan to depth of ¼ in. (6 mm). Fry trout over medium heat until crisp and brown on both sides (5-10 minutes per side). Serve immediately.

Serves 4.

BAKED STUFFED SALMON	2-2½ kg . 4-6 lb	dressed salmon, preferably with backbone removed
	50 gm . 2 oz	butter
	½	onion, minced
	4 tbsp	chopped parsley
	¼ tsp	marjoram
	⅛ tsp	pepper
	½ tsp	salt
	225 gm . 8 oz	soft breadcrumbs
	2 tbsp	water

Fry onion in butter until tender and golden. Add parsley, marjoram, pepper, salt and breadcrumbs and mix well. Stir in water. Sprinkle inside of salmon with salt and pepper and spoon stuffing into cavity. Fasten with skewers or toothpicks and lace with twine. Bake in a moderate oven (350° F, 180°C, Gas Mark 4) until the thick part of the salmon can be easily flaked with a fork. It should not be dry. Cooking time will depend on size of fish, about 18 minutes per pound (20 minutes per half-kilo).

Serves 8 — 10.

SALMON LOAF NO. 1	450 gm . 1 lb	tinned salmon
	70 ml . ½ gill	liquid from salmon
	140 ml . 1 gill	milk
	2	eggs, beaten
	140 gm . 5 oz	soft breadcrumbs
	2 tbsp	chopped onion
	½ stick	celery, finely chopped
	1 tsp	salt
	¼ tsp	pepper

Drain salmon, saving ½ gill (70 ml) of liquid. Discard skin and bones and mash salmon with fork. Combine salmon liquid, milk and breadcrumbs and leave to stand 5 minutes. Add remaining ingredients and mix well. Turn into greased loaf tin or ovenproof dish and bake in a moderate oven (350° F, 180°C, Gas Mark 4) for 35 minutes or until lightly browned. Serve with Parsley Sauce (see p. 157).

Serves 6.

SALMON LOAF NO. 2	250 gm . 8-10 oz	cooked fresh salmon, bones and skin removed
	140 gm . 5 oz	soft breadcrumbs
	200 ml . 1½ gills	milk
	2	eggs, beaten
	1½ tsp	salt
	¼ tsp	pepper
	2 tbsp	chopped onion
	½ stick	celery, finely chopped

Combine all ingredients and mix well. Turn into greased loaf tin or oven-proof dish. Bake in a moderate oven (350°F, 180°C, Gas Mark 4) for 35 minutes. Serve with Parsley Sauce (see p. 157).

Serves 4.

TUNA CASSEROLE			
100 gm	.	4 oz	macaroni pieces
350 gm	.	12 oz	tinned tuna fish, drained
		4 tbsp	butter
50 gm	.	2 oz	chopped mushrooms
		4 tbsp	flour
365 ml	.	⅔ pt	milk
		½ tsp	salt
		¼ tsp	pepper
225 gm	.	8 oz	frozen peas
50 gm	.	2 oz	grated cheese

Cook macaroni in boiling water until tender. Drain. Melt butter and fry mushrooms until tender. Stir in flour. Gradually add milk, salt and pepper and cook over low heat, stirring, until mixture is thickened. Add tuna. Cook peas in boiling water until tender and combine with macaroni and tuna mixture. Mix well and turn into a buttered ovenproof dish. Sprinkle with cheese. Bake in a moderate oven (375°F, 190°C, Gas Mark 5) for 30 minutes.

Serves 4.

TUNA RICE RING			
225 gm	.	8 oz	white rice
1½ l	.	3 pt	cold water
2 tsp	.	2½ tsp	salt
		4 tbsp	chopped black olives
		3 tbsp	chopped celery
85 gm	.	3 oz	grated Cheddar cheese
175 gm	.	6 oz	tinned tuna fish, drained
285 gm	.	10 oz	tinned condensed cream of mushroom or cream of chicken soup

Combine rice, water and salt in saucepan and bring to boil. Simmer, uncovered, 10 minutes. Drain. Add olives, celery and cheese and mix well. Pack into a buttered ring-shaped mould and bake in a slow oven (300°F, 150°C, Gas Mark 2) for 10 minutes. Unmould onto a serving platter. Heat tuna with undiluted soup and turn into centre of ring.

Chicken Rice Ring

Substitute 8 oz (225 gm) cooked boneless chicken for tuna in above recipe.

Vegetable Rice Ring

Prepare rice ring as above but fill centre with mixture of cooked vegetables, such as peas, corn or spinach, and White Sauce or Parsley Sauce (see p. 157).

SHRIMP
COCKTAIL

140 ml . 1 gill	ketchup
2 tbsp	lemon juice
2 tbsp	horseradish sauce
1 tsp	Worcestershire sauce
¼ tsp	salt
⅛ tsp	pepper
225 gm . 8 oz	cooked shelled shrimps

Combine ketchup with all other ingredients except shrimps and mix well. Chill thoroughly. Divide shrimps among six cocktail glasses and pour sauce over them.

Crab Cocktail

Use cooked crab meat in place of shrimps in above recipe.

SHRIMP WIGGLE

3 tbsp	butter or margarine
3 tbsp	plain flour
400 ml . ¾ pt	milk
½ tsp	salt
¼ tsp	pepper
75 gm . 3 oz	Cheddar cheese, cubed
170 gm . 6 oz	cooked, shelled shrimps

Melt butter and stir in flour. Gradually add milk. Add salt, pepper and cheese and cook, stirring, until thickened and smooth. Add shrimps and continue cooking 5 minutes, stirring constantly. Serve over toast.
    Serves 4.

SEAFOOD	350 gm . 12 oz	cooked crab, tuna or shrimps or a
CASSEROLE		combination
	4 tbsp	butter
	4 tbsp	chopped onion
	½ stick	celery, chopped
	125 gm . 4 oz	sliced mushrooms
	5 tbsp	plain flour
	275 ml . ½ pt	milk
	½ tsp	salt
	¼ tsp	pepper
	2 tbsp	chopped parsley
	50 gm . 2 oz	grated Cheddar cheese

Melt butter and fry onion, celery and mushrooms until tender. Stir in flour and add milk, salt and pepper. Cook over low heat, stirring, until thickened. Add seafood and parsley and turn into ovenproof dish. Sprinkle cheese over top and place under hot grill until cheese is golden-brown.
    Serves 4.

SCALLOPED	550 ml . 1 pt fresh	
OYSTERS	or	oysters
	450 gm . 1 lb tinned	
	140 ml . 1 gill	liquid from oysters
	50 gm . 2 oz	butter
	115 gm . 4 oz	fine cracker crumbs
	½ tsp	salt
	4 tbsp	chopped parsley
	140 ml . 1 gill	evaporated milk
	1 tsp	Worcestershire sauce
	⅛ tsp	cayenne pepper
		paprika

Melt butter and combine with crumbs, salt and parsley. Spread half of mixture in ovenproof dish. Spoon drained oysters over. Cover with remaining crumb mixture. Mix oyster liquid, evaporated milk, Worcestershire sauce, and cayenne and pour over. Bake in a moderate oven (350°F, 180°C, Gas Mark 4) for 30 minutes. Sprinkle with paprika.
    Serves 4.

OYSTERS IN		
BARBECUE		
SAUCE	550 ml . 1 pt fresh	
	or	oysters, drained
	450 gm . 1 lb tinned	
	275 ml . ½ pt	Red Barbecue Sauce
		(see p. 110)

Arrange oysters in buttered shallow ovenproof dish. Pour sauce over them. Bake in a moderate oven (375°F, 190°C, Gas Mark 5), basting frequently, for 30 minutes.

Serves 4.

PAN-FRIED OYSTERS

2 dozen	large oysters
	salt and pepper
1	egg, beaten
	cracker crumbs, finely crushed
4 tbsp	cooking fat or butter

Sprinkle oysters lightly with salt and pepper. Dip each one in beaten egg and coat with cracker crumbs. Fry until crisp and brown on both sides.

Serves 4 — 6.

HANGTOWN FRY

6 rashers	streaky bacon, cut in half
12	oysters, medium size
6	eggs
3 tbsp	milk
½ tsp	salt
⅛ tsp	pepper

Fry bacon until crisp. Drain on paper towels. Pour off all but 2 tablespoons of drippings. Fry oysters in the fat until brown on both sides. Beat eggs with milk, salt and pepper and pour over oysters. Cook over low heat, without stirring, until set on top and brown on bottom. Slide carefully out of frying pan onto a heated platter and serve with the bacon.

Serves 4.

OYSTER STEW

550 ml . 1 pt fresh *or*	oysters with
450 gm . 1 lb tinned	liquid
4 tbsp	butter
2 tbsp	plain flour
1 tsp	salt
¼ tsp	pepper
1 tsp	Worcestershire sauce
550 ml . 1 pt	milk
	butter

Melt butter over low heat and stir in flour. Gradually stir in oyster liquid. Add oysters, salt, pepper and Worcestershire sauce, and bring to boil over low heat. Simmer *gently* 5 minutes. Add milk and heat but *do not boil.* Place a pat of butter on top of each serving.
    Serves 3.

OREGON CLAM CHOWDER

340 gm .	12 oz	potatoes, peeled and diced
180 ml .	⅓ pt	water
50 gm .	2 oz	streaky bacon, diced
	1	onion, chopped
	2 tbsp	plain flour
400 ml .	¾ pt	milk
	1 tsp	salt
	¼ tsp	pepper
340 gm .	12 oz	tinned minced clams with liquid

Cook potatoes in water until tender. Fry bacon with onion until tender. Stir in flour. Add potatoes and cooking liquid, milk, salt, pepper and clams with liquid. Heat, stirring, until thickened. Serve with crackers.
    Serves 4.

CRAB LOUIS

340 gm . 12 oz	cooked crab meat, fresh, frozen or tinned
1 large head	lettuce
4 large	tomatoes, cut into wedges
4	hard-boiled eggs, quartered
	salt
12	black olives, stoned
	Louis Dressing, or other salad dressing if preferred

Drain crab meat if tinned. Reserve a few large pieces and flake remainder with a fork. Place 2 large lettuce leaves on each of four salad plates. Shred remainder of lettuce and place on the leaves. Arrange flaked crab meat on top, sprinkle lightly with salt, and pour a small amount of Louis Dressing over each salad. Place large pieces of crab on top and arrange tomato wedges, eggs and olives around the edge. Pass remaining salad dressing.
    Serves 4.

Shrimp Louis

Use cooked shrimps in place of crab meat in above recipe.

LOUIS	140 ml . 1 gill	mayonnaise
DRESSING	70 ml . ½ gill	ketchup
	1	spring onion, chopped
	1 tsp	Worcestershire sauce
	½ tsp	salt
	¼ tsp	pepper

Combine and mix well. Chill 1 hour. Serve with Crab Louis or Shrimp Louis.

WESTERN	170 gm . 6 oz	dry red beans or
CHILLI		haricot beans
	1 tbsp	salad oil
	450 gm . 1 lb	minced raw beef
	1	onion, chopped
	1	green pepper, chopped
	1 clove	garlic, crushed
	2 tbsp	plain flour
	275 ml . ½ pt	water
	450 gm . 1 lb	tinned tomatoes
	225 gm . 8 oz	tinned tomato purée
	1 tsp	salt
	¼ tsp	pepper
	2 tbsp	chilli powder

Soak beans overnight in cold water. Drain. Add fresh water to cover and bring to boil. Simmer, covered, until tender (about 1 hour). Heat oil in large heavy saucepan. Add beef, breaking it up well, onion, green pepper and garlic. Cook, stirring occasionally, 10-15 minutes. Skim off excess fat. Stir in flour. Gradually add water, tomatoes, purée, salt, pepper, chilli and cooked beans. Simmer gently 45 minutes, stirring occasionally.
    Serves 6 — 8.

CHUCKWAGON	4 rashers	streaky bacon
BEEF AND BEANS	1 large	onion, chopped
	1 stick	celery, chopped
	450 gm . 1 lb	minced raw beef
	1 tbsp	plain flour
	½ tsp	salt
	½ tsp	pepper
	140 ml . 1 gill	tomato ketchup
	900 gm . 2 lb	tinned baked beans

Fry bacon until crisp and remove from pan. Drain off all but 2 tablespoons of the fat. Add onion, celery and beef and cook, stirring, until meat is lightly browned and vegetables are tender. Stir in flour, salt, pepper, ketchup and beans and mix well. Pour into an ovenproof dish and lay bacon slices over the top. Bake in a very moderate oven (325°F, 170°C, Gas Mark 3) for 20 minutes.

Serves 6 — 8.

PEPPER STEAK	450 gm . 1 lb	stewing beef steak
	¾ tsp	salt
	⅛ tsp	pepper
	1 tbsp	cooking fat
	1 large	onion, chopped
	1 clove	garlic, crushed
	140 ml . 1 gill	water
	2 tbsp	soy sauce
	1 large	green pepper, cut into strips
	1½ tbsp	cornflour
	70 ml . ½ gill	cold water
	1 large	tomato, peeled and cut into wedges

Cut meat into small thin strips, sprinkle with salt and pepper and fry with onion and garlic in hot fat until browned. Add water and soy sauce and simmer, covered, until tender (1½ to 2 hours). Add green pepper and simmer 5 minutes. Mix cornflour with cold water and stir into mixture. Cook, stirring, until thickened. Add tomato wedges and simmer 5 minutes. Serve over rice.

Serves 4.

PORK CHOP SUEY	450 gm . 1 lb	lean boneless pork
	125 gm . 4 oz	sliced mushrooms
	2 sticks	celery, sliced
	1 large	onion, sliced
	365 ml . ⅔ pt	water
	2	beef stock cubes
	450 gm . 1 lb	tinned bean sprouts, drained and rinsed
	3 tbsp	soy sauce
	3 tbsp	cold water
	3 tbsp	cornflour
		boiled rice

Cut pork into small thin strips and brown in large frying pan. Add mushrooms, celery and onion and cook and stir over high heat 3 minutes. Add water and beef cubes and simmer 20 minutes. Add bean sprouts. Mix soy sauce, cold water and cornflour into a smooth paste and stir into pork and vegetable mixture. Cook, stirring, until thickened. Serve over hot rice.

Shrimp Chop Suey

Use 1 lb (450 gm) shelled shrimps and 2 tablespoons butter in place of pork.

CHINESE	*225 gm* . 8 oz	lean boneless pork
PEAPODS WITH	1 tbsp	cooking oil
PORK	*115 gm* . 4 oz	sliced mushrooms
	225 gm . 8 oz	tinned water chestnuts, sliced
	100 gm . 4 oz	tinned bamboo shoots, sliced
	1 stick	celery, sliced
	1	green pepper, cut into thin strips
	275 ml . ½ pt	water
	2 tbsp	soy sauce
	½ tsp	ginger
	2	chicken stock cubes
	225 gm . 8 oz	Chinese peapods, fresh
		or frozen
	2 tbsp	cornflour
	70 ml . ½ gill	cold water

Cut pork into very thin strips and fry quickly in hot oil. Add mushrooms, drained water chestnuts and bamboo shoots, celery and green pepper. Add water, soy sauce, ginger, and stock cubes, lower heat and simmer, covered, 15 minutes. Add peapods and cook 5 minutes. Mix cornflour and cold water and add to mixture. Cook and stir until thick. Serve immediately with rice.
    Serves 6.

SWEET AND	*900 gm* . 2 lb	pork chops, cut thin
SOUR PORK	2 tbsp	brown sugar
	½ tsp	salt
	3 tbsp	cornflour
	3 tbsp	vinegar
	1 tbsp	soy sauce
	400 ml . ¾ pt	water
	1	green pepper, chopped
	1	onion, chopped
	225 gm . 8 oz	tinned crushed pineapple,
		with juice

Fry chops slowly until well browned on both sides. Drain off fat. Mix sugar, salt, cornflour, vinegar and soy sauce with the water and pineapple. Pour over chops and simmer gently, stirring frequently, for 20 minutes. Add green pepper and onion and continue cooking for 20 minutes longer.
    Serves 4.

BOILED RICE

150 gm .	6 oz	white rice
1½ l. .	3 pt	cold water
	1 tbsp	salt

Combine in large saucepan and bring to boil. Lower heat slightly and keep mixture at slow boil for exactly 10 minutes. Strain through a colander and serve at once.

VENISON ROAST

2½ kg .	5-6 lb	venison
	2 cloves	garlic, crushed
	¼ tsp	pepper
170 gm .	6 oz	streaky bacon

Trim all fat from venison. Rub crushed garlic and pepper over meat and place on large square of heavy aluminium foil. Place strips of bacon over top and wrap tightly in the foil. Place in baking tin and bake in a very moderate oven (325°F, 170°C, Gas Mark 3) for 4 hours.

ALASKAN BEAR STEW

50 gm .	2 oz	streaky bacon, diced
	2	onions, chopped
900 gm .	2 lb	boneless lean bear meat
	1 clove	garlic, crushed
	4 tbsp	plain flour
550 ml .	1 pt	water
140 ml .	1 gill	sherry
	¼ tsp	pepper
	dash	cayenne pepper
	¼ tsp	cloves
	¼ tsp	oregano
350 gm .	12 oz	carrots, sliced
350 gm .	12 oz	potatoes, cubed
		salt

Fry bacon and onion together 5 minutes. Add bear meat and garlic and cook until brown. Stir in flour. Add water, sherry, pepper, cayenne, cloves and oregano. Simmer, covered, stirring occasionally, until meat is tender (1-2 hours). Add carrots, potatoes and salt to taste. Continue cooking until vegetables are tender.
Serves 6 — 8.

Frontier Beef Stew

Use boneless lean stewing beef in place of bear meat in above recipe.

BUFFALO	675 gm . 1½ lb	raw minced buffalo meat
LOAF	85 gm . 3 oz	breadcrumbs
	2	eggs
	200 ml . 1½ gills	tomato purée
	½	onion, finely chopped
	1 tsp	salt
	¼ tsp	pepper
	¼ tsp	basil

Combine all ingredients and mix well. Shape into a loaf and place in a baking tin. Bake in a moderate oven (350°F, 180°C, Gas Mark 4) for 60-70 minutes.
Serves 6 — 8.

Beef Loaf

Use minced raw beef in place of buffalo meat in above recipe.

FRIED RABBIT	1	rabbit, cut into joints
	50 gm . 2 oz	plain flour
	2 tsp	salt
	½ tsp	pepper
		fat or oil for frying

Mix flour, salt and pepper and coat rabbit pieces with mixture. Heat fat or oil in large frying pan to depth of ⅛ in. (3 mm). Add rabbit pieces and fry until well browned on both sides. Pour off excess fat, cover frying pan, and cook over low heat 30 minutes. Remove cover and raise heat for 5 minutes.

RABBIT	1	rabbit
FRICASSEE		flour
		salt, pepper
	4 tbsp	butter
	2 tbsp	plain flour
	275 ml . ½ pt	dry red wine
	1	onion, chopped

1 stick	celery, chopped
1	chicken stock cube
¼ tsp	thyme

Cut rabbit into joints and dust with flour. Sprinkle with salt and pepper. Fry in butter until browned on all sides. Remove rabbit pieces to an ovenproof dish. Fry onion and celery in same frying pan until tender. Stir in flour and slowly add wine. Add chicken cube and thyme and cook, stirring, until mixture bubbles. Pour wine mixture over rabbit, cover dish, and bake in a very moderate oven (325°F, 170°C, Gas Mark 3) for 2 hours.

Serves 4.

CRAB AND CHEESE SANDWICHES

8 slices	bread, buttered
115 gm . 4 oz	cooked crab meat
2 tbsp	mayonnaise
1 tsp	lemon juice
4 slices	cheese

Lay four slices bread in large frying pan, buttered side down. Mix crab with mayonnaise and lemon juice and spread on bread. Top with cheese slices and remaining bread slices, buttered side up. Fry over medium heat until bread is browned on both sides and cheese is melted.

4 sandwiches.

Tuna-Cheese Sandwiches

Substitute 6-oz (175-gm) tin tuna fish, drained, for crab in above recipe.

DENVER SANDWICHES

4	eggs
¼	green pepper, chopped
¼	onion, chopped
50 gm . 2 oz	chopped cooked ham
½ tsp	salt
dash	pepper
8 slices	bread, toasted and buttered

Beat eggs and mix with green pepper, onion, ham, salt and pepper. Pour into hot buttered frying pan and cook over medium heat until set. Turn and cook for 2 minutes on other side. Cut into quarters and place each piece between two slices of buttered toast.

4 sandwiches.

REUBEN SANDWICHES

70 ml .	½ gill	mayonnaise
	2 tsp	ketchup
	8 slices	bread
170 gm .	6 oz	cooked boiled beef, thinly sliced
170 gm .	6 oz	Gruyère cheese, sliced
275 ml .	½ pt	sauerkraut
		butter

Mix mayonnaise with ketchup and spread on bread slices. Top four of the slices with sliced beef and cheese. Drain sauerkraut, rinse with cold water, and drain again. Place sauerkraut on top of cheese and top with remaining bread slices. Spread outsides of sandwiches with butter and fry or grill slowly on both sides until browned and heated through. Serve immediately.
    4 sandwiches.

GREEN GODDESS SALAD

1 head	lettuce, torn into small pieces
1 large	tomato, cut into thin wedges
6	black olives, stoned and sliced
	Green Goddess Salad
	Dressing

Combine lettuce, tomato and olives and arrange on four salad plates. Pour Green Goddess Salad Dressing over.

GREEN GODDESS SALAD DRESSING

9 tbsp	mayonnaise
3 tbsp	vinegar
2 tbsp	finely chopped chives
2 tbsp	chopped parsley
1	spring onion, finely chopped
¼ tsp	crushed tarragon
dash	pepper
¼ tsp	salt
4	anchovy fillets, chopped very fine
4 tbsp	milk

Combine all ingredients and mix well. Chill several hours.

CAESAR SALAD

5 tbsp	olive oil or salad oil
4 tbsp	vinegar
1 clove	garlic, crushed
2 tsp	Worcestershire sauce
¼ tsp	salt
dash	pepper
1	raw egg

1 head	lettuce, torn into small pieces
	Croutons
8 tbsp	grated Parmesan cheese
2 tbsp	crumbled blue cheese

Mix first seven ingredients thoroughly and chill. Combine lettuce, croutons and cheeses and pour dressing over them. Toss lightly and serve immediately.

Serves 8.

CROUTONS

Spread 3 slices bread cut into small cubes on a baking sheet and bake in a moderate oven (350°F, 180°C, Gas Mark 4) for 15 minutes or until brown and crisp. Cool and store in covered container. Use as garnish for salad or soup.

DE LUXE CROUTONS

4 slices	bread, cubed
2 tbsp	butter, melted
1 tsp	grated Parmesan cheese
¼ tsp	powdered garlic

Toss bread cubes in melted butter until butter is absorbed. Sprinkle with Parmesan and garlic powder and mix well. Spread on a baking sheet and bake in a moderate oven (350°F, 180°C, Gas Mark 4) for 20 minutes or until brown and crisp. Store in covered container. Use on salads or soups.

WESTERN SALAD BAR

On a serving counter arrange a large bowl of lettuce, torn into small pieces, and dishes of the following:

   diced celery
   diced beetroot
   chopped spring onions
   cherry-sized tomatoes, or tomato wedges
   chickpeas, cooked or tinned, drained
   Blue Cheese Salad Dressing
   French Dressing
   Ranch-Style Salad Dressing
   Croutons

Place a stack of chilled plates nearby and allow guests to combine their own salads with choice of dressing.

BLUE CHEESE	5 tbsp	evaporated milk
SALAD	5 tbsp	salad oil
DRESSING	2 tbsp	vinegar
	1 tbsp	lemon juice
	¼ tsp	mustard powder
	½ tsp	salt
	¼ tsp	pepper
	½ tsp	sugar
	6 tbsp	crumbled blue cheese

Combine in a jar and shake well. Chill thoroughly. Shake again before serving.

FRENCH	9 tbsp	salad oil
DRESSING	3 tbsp	vinegar
	2 tbsp	lemon juice
	½ tsp	salt
	speck	black pepper
	¼ tsp	mustard powder
	¼ tsp	paprika

Combine in a jar and shake well. Refrigerate. Shake before using.

RANCH-STYLE		¾ tsp	salt
SALAD		1 tbsp	finely chopped parsley
DRESSING		¼ tsp	powdered garlic
		½ tsp	pepper
		1 tsp	minced onion
		½ tsp	minced chives
		¼ tsp	crushed tarragon
	140 ml . 1 gill	mayonnaise
	140 ml . 1 gill	buttermilk

Combine all ingredients and mix thoroughly. Chill.

SOURDOUGH	*450 gm* . 1 lb	Sourdough Starter
BREAD		(see p. 68)
	450 gm . 1 lb	plain flour
	1½ tbsp	cooking oil
	1 tsp	salt
	½ tsp	bicarbonate of soda
	140 ml . 1 gill	lukewarm water

Combine Starter with about 2 oz (50 gm) of the flour, the salt, soda and oil, and mix well. Stir in water. Add 8 oz (225 gm) flour, a little at a time. Pour remaining flour onto a board and turn dough onto it. Knead well for 15 minutes, adding the flour only as needed to prevent stickiness. Place doughball in clean buttered basin, turning to grease all surfaces, cover with a cloth and leave in a warm place until doubled in bulk (about 4 hours). Punch down and divide into two oval loaves. Place side by side in greased 8-in. (20-cm) square baking tin. Cover and leave again to raise until doubled. Bake in moderate oven (375°F, 190°C, Gas Mark 5) for 1 hour. If bread browns too quickly, cover lightly with a piece of aluminium foil. Break loaves apart.

SOURDOUGH PANCAKES

275 ml . ½ pt	Sourdough Starter (see p. 68)	
115 gm . 4 oz	plain flour	
3 tbsp	sugar	
¾ tsp	salt	
½ tsp	bicarbonate of soda	
4 tbsp	evaporated milk	
4 tbsp	water	
1	egg	
3 tbsp	melted butter	

Stir Starter and measure into basin. Combine flour, sugar, salt and bicarbonate of soda. Beat egg with milk and water and combine with melted butter; add to Starter. Stir in flour mixture and mix well. Spoon 5 tablespoons of mixture onto hot, lightly greased griddle or frying pan and cook until bottom is brown and top is bubbly and beginning to look dry. Turn and brown other side. Serve with butter and syrup, honey or jam.

10 — 12 pancakes.

SOURDOUGH BISCUITS

225 gm . 8 oz	plain flour	
2¼ tsp	baking powder	
¾ tsp	salt	
180 ml . ⅓ pt	Sourdough Starter (see p. 68)	
3 tbsp	salad oil	
4 tbsp	milk	

Sieve 7 oz (200 gm) of the flour with baking powder and salt. Stir Starter before measuring into a basin. Add oil and milk to Starter and stir in flour mixture. Pour remaining flour onto a board and turn dough onto it. Knead well for 5 minutes. Roll to ½-in. (12-mm) thickness and cut into 2-in. (5-cm) rounds. Bake in a moderately hot oven (400°F, 200°C, Gas Mark 6) for 20 minutes. Serve warm with butter and jam.

12 biscuits.

SOURDOUGH STARTER

7 gm .	¼ oz	active dry yeast
	8 tbsp	lukewarm water
	4 tbsp	sugar
	2 tbsp	vinegar
	2 tsp	salt
450 gm .	1 lb	plain flour
365 ml .	⅔ pt	warm water

Dissolve yeast in 8 tablespoons of warm water. Stir in sugar, vinegar and salt and add flour gradually; mix well. Add the warm water gradually, mixing to a smooth batter. Place in a glass or ceramic basin and cover with a plate or cloth. Leave in a warm place to ferment for at least 48 hours.

To use: Remove 1 lb (450 gm) of the Starter and use as required. To remaining Starter add 8 oz (225 gm) plain flour and ½ pt (275 ml) warm water. Beat until smooth, cover with plate and leave in warm place 48 hours before using again. If Starter is not used within a week, store in refrigerator. Allow to warm to room temperature before using and replenishing. Always stir Starter before using.

Note: Do not use metal spoons or basins for sourdough recipes.

BAKED ALASKA

	1 layer	plain white cake, baked in sandwich tin and cooled
800 ml .	1½ pt	ice cream
	4	egg whites
	¼ tsp	cream of tartar
100 gm .	3½ oz	sugar

Pack ice cream into shallow round dish, slightly smaller than cake. Place in freezer for 1 hour. Place cake on ovenproof plate and unmould ice cream on top of it. Return to freezer. Beat egg whites with cream of tartar until soft peaks form. Beat in the sugar 1 tablespoon at a time and continue beating until stiff. Spread meringue over ice cream and cake, covering completely the top and sides. Cake may be returned to freezer until serving time (up to 24 hours).

To serve: Place cake in bottom of a hot oven (450°F, 230°C, Gas Mark 8) just until lightly browned (nor more than 5 minutes). Serve immediately.

Serves 10.

WESTERN COFFEE CAKE

150 gm .	6 oz	sugar
50 gm .	2 oz	butter or margarine
	1	egg
125 ml .	1 gill	milk
175 gm .	7 oz	plain flour
1¾ tsp .	2 tsp	baking powder

¼ tsp	salt	
50 gm . 2 oz	raisins	

Topping	2 tbsp	sugar
	1 tsp	cinnamon

Combine sugar, butter and egg and mix well. Stir in milk. Sieve together flour, baking powder and salt and add to first mixture with the raisins. Mix well and pour into a greased 9-in. (23-cm) square baking tin. Mix sugar and cinnamon for Topping and sprinkle over batter. Bake in a moderate oven (375°F, 190°C, Gas Mark 5) for 25 minutes. Cut into squares and serve warm.

GRANOLA

225 gm . 8 oz	rolled oats
115 gm . 4 oz	brown sugar
40 gm . 1½ oz	desiccated coconut
40 gm . 1½ oz	sunflower seeds or sesame seeds
40 gm . 1½ oz	raisins
25 gm . 1 oz	wheat germ
1 tsp	cinnamon
40 gm . 1½ oz	butter

Combine all ingredients and spread in a shallow baking tin. Bake in a moderate oven (350°F, 180°C, Gas Mark 4) for 20 minutes. Cool. Store in covered container. Serve as a breakfast cereal with cold milk or cream.

SAN FRANCISCO IRISH COFFEE

Irish whiskey
brown sugar
hot coffee
unsweetened whipped cream

In a goblet or glass place 3 tablespoons Irish whiskey and 1 teaspoon brown sugar. Pour hot coffee into glass, leaving space at top. Stir. Place heaped tablespoon of whipped cream on top but *do not stir*. Serve immediately.

Hawaii

LUAUS AND FLOWER LEIS

The newest of the United States is a tropical beauty. Hawaii became the 50th state of the Union in 1959. Although there are over one hundred islands in the Hawaiian chain, stretching across two thousand miles of Pacific Ocean, only eight can be considered major islands, and most tourists see only four of those: Oahu, Hawaii, Maui, and Kauai. Island-hopping jet planes whisk passengers from island to island in minutes.

Hawaii is a land of contrasts: giant waves and quiet lagoons; flower-filled valleys and stark lava beds; sheer, wind-swept *pali* cliffs above sun-drenched fields of pineapples and sugar cane; white-sand beach at Waikiki and black-sand beach at Kalapana; sprawling metropolis of Honolulu and roadless tree-fern jungles. But the warm air, the fragrance of plumeria and ginger blossom, and the soft, lingering melodies of the guitar, are everywhere.

The Polynesians, the true Hawaiians, are dark-skinned, dark-eyed and tall, but few remain. Most Hawaiians today are a blend of Oriental, European and Polynesian. The food in Hawaii reflects the various cultures and traditions, but it also reflects the tropical climate. Sugar cane and pineapples are important crops. Papayas (paw-paws), mangoes, coconuts, avocadoes and bananas flourish. From the taro plant come spinach-like taro leaves and *poi*, a paste made by pulverizing the root. Plantations on the big island of Hawaii provide Kona coffee and Macadamia nuts. For the intrepid hunter there are fierce wild boars as well as deer and goats. Beef, pork and poultry are produced on the ranches. The warm blue seas surrounding the islands swarm with hundreds of varieties of fish from giant marlin weighing more than a thousand pounds to tiny angel fish swimming among the coral.

Festivals in Hawaii include Aloha Week in late summer, Chinese New Year, Lei Day (1 May) and Kamehameha Day, but any day can be Luau Day. Luau means simply 'big feast' and the traditional luau began with the digging of the *imu* or pit. Hot rocks were piled into the bottom of the pit, then covered with a layer of *ti* leaves (the same leaves used to make the grass skirts). A pig, stuffed with more hot rocks, was lowered into the pit, covered with another layer of hot rocks and leaves and a final covering of earth. Many hours later, the Kalua Pig was ready to serve, meat falling from the bones in moist, tender shreds, smoky-fragrant and delicious. *Laulaus* — packages of yams, bananas, fish and chicken wrapped in taro leaves — were baked in the imu along with the pig. To complete the feast were Poi, Lomi Lomi (raw salmon mixed with salt, onions and tomatoes), Haupia (coconut pudding), and a variety of fresh fruits such as pineapples, papayas, mangoes, and bananas. Guests sat on the ground for the feast and the eating and drinking, singing and dancing, lasted for days.

Today, most hotels in Hawaii have a Luau night. The buffet-style dinner includes the traditional foods but it is eaten at tables decorated with plumeria blossoms and orchids and whole pineapples. Guests wear colourful muumuu dresses and Aloha shirts, and there are flower leis for the ladies. The entertainment following the dinner includes the graceful Hawaiian hula, the frenzied Samoan fire-dance, and the music, songs and dances of the Maoris, Tahitians, and Fijis.

While cooking in a pit is beyond the facilities of most kitchens, and raw fish is not acceptable to many Haoles (non Hawaiians), a Luau is not an impossibility, even in a suburban back garden or city flat. Guests can be invited to wear colourful dresses and shirts, and the house can be decorated with plenty of flowers (paper, if necessary) and fresh fruit piled in the centre of the buffet table. The recipes here are simple to prepare and will taste surprisingly authentic. Poi is packed in jars in Hawaii and is available in some speciality shops. One jar will go a long way at a Haole Luau. It takes a native Hawaiian really to appreciate it.

OVEN KALUA PIG

2¼ kg .	5 lb	boneless pork leg
	1 tbsp	liquid smoke (if available)
	2 tbsp	salt

Rub liquid smoke and salt into pork and wrap meat tightly in aluminium foil. Bake in a moderate oven (350°F, 180°C, Gas Mark 4) for 5 hours. Shred meat and pile on a platter.

Serves 12.

HULI HULI CHICKEN

1 kg .	2½ lb	frying chicken, cut into joints
50 gm .	2 oz	butter, melted
3½ tbsp .	4 tbsp	soy sauce
	1 tsp	sugar
	½ tsp	ground ginger

Lay chicken pieces, skin side down, on a grill pan. Mix remaining ingredients and brush surface of chicken liberally with mixture. Grill until well browned. Turn chicken and brush other side with mixture. Grill until well browned. Bake in a very slow oven (275°F, 135°C, Gas Mark 1) for 1 hour.

Serves 4.

ISLAND CHICKEN SALAD

450 gm .	1 lb	boneless cooked chicken, chopped
	3 sticks	celery, diced
	1 small	cooking apple, peeled, cored and diced
25 gm .	1 oz	finely chopped nuts
225 gm .	8 oz	tinned crushed pineapple, drained
275 ml .	½ pt	mayonnaise
	2 tsp	curry powder
	¼ tsp	ground ginger
	¼ tsp	salt

Combine chicken with celery, apple and nuts. Mix pineapple with remaining ingredients and add to chicken mixture. Mix well and chill 2-3 hours. Serve on lettuce leaves.

Serves 8.

LOMI LOMI

675 gm .	1½ lb	salmon
	3	tomatoes, diced
	1	onion, chopped
	5	spring onion, chopped
70 ml .	½ gill	water
	1 tsp	salt

Cook salmon by baking or steaming. Remove skin and bones and shred salmon with a fork. Combine with remaining ingredients and mix well. Chill several hours.

12 small servings.

BAKED FISH

900 gm .	2 lb	fish fillets
	2 tbsp	lemon juice
	4 tbsp	mayonnaise
	1 tsp	soy sauce
75 gm .	3 oz	cornflakes, finely crushed
75 gm .	3 oz	finely chopped almonds
	1 tsp	salt
	⅛ tsp	pepper

Combine lemon juice, mayonnaise and soy sauce and coat each fillet with mixture. Mix cornflake crumbs, nuts, salt and pepper and roll the coated fillets in crumb mixture. Lay the fish fillets in a greased baking tin and bake in a moderate oven (350°F, 180°C, Gas Mark 4) for 30 minutes.

Serves 6.

HAWAIIAN- STYLE YAMS	1¼ kg . 3 lb	yams or sweet potatoes
	100 gm . 4 oz	butter
	200 gm . 8 oz	brown sugar
	125 ml . 1 gill	water
	40 gm . 1½ oz	desiccated coconut

Cook yams or sweet potatoes in boiling water until barely tender. Peel and cut into thick slices. Mix butter, brown sugar and water and cook over medium heat until thick. Lower heat, add yams, and simmer gently 10 minutes. Pour into a serving dish and sprinkle with coconut.
Serves 12.

BAKED BANANAS	12	firm bananas
	25 gm . 1 oz	desiccated coconut
	50 gm . 2 oz	sugar
	125 ml . 1 gill	water
	1	lime (juice)

Peel bananas and lay in a buttered baking tin. Mix coconut, sugar, water and lime juice and bring to boil. Simmer 3 minutes and pour over bananas. Bake in a moderate oven (350°F, 180°C, Gas Mark 4) for 30 minutes.
Serves 12.

FRIED BANANAS	4	very firm bananas
	1 tbsp	lemon juice
	4 tbsp	butter
	1 tsp	cinnamon
	2 tbsp	sugar

Peel bananas and cut in halves lengthwise. Sprinkle with lemon juice. Heat butter in frying pan and fry bananas in butter until browned on both sides. Sprinkle with cinnamon and sugar.
Serves 4.

HAWAIIAN FRUIT SALAD	450 gm . 1 lb	pineapple chunks, drained
	450 gm . 1 lb	tinned mandarin oranges, drained
	1	ripe papaya (paw-paw) or 2 fresh peaches, peeled, diced
	2	bananas, sliced
	40 gm . 1½ oz	desiccated coconut
	50 gm . 2 oz	miniature marshmallows
	1½ tbsp	lime or lemon juice
	2 tbsp	sweet condensed milk

Combine fruits with marshmallows and coconut. Mix juice with condensed milk and combine with fruit. Chill several hours.

Serves 12.

LUAU PINEAPPLE

1 large	fresh ripe pineapple, with leaves attached

Cut pineapple lengthwise (including leaves) into two halves. Cut out the core and discard. Cut the fruit out in chunks, leaving shell ½ in. (12 mm) thick. Pile fruit chunks loosely back into the shells.

HAWAIIAN DELIGHT

Coconut Layer

1 l.	1 qt	milk
75 gm	3 oz	desiccated coconut
150 gm	6 oz	sugar
50 gm	2 oz	cornflour
	½ tsp	salt
	1 tsp	almond essence

Mix coconut, sugar, cornflour and salt with 5 tablespoons of milk. Stir in remaining milk and cook, stirring, over low heat until thickened. Stir in almond essence. Cool partially. Pour into large glass dish. Chill.

Pineapple-Rum Layer

565 gm	20 oz	tinned crushed pineapple
	1½ tbsp	cornflour
	6 tbsp	rum
	½ tsp	ginger

Mix 2 tablespoons of juice from pineapple with cornflour in saucepan. Add rum, pineapple and remaining juice, and ginger. Cook, stirring, over low heat until thickened. Cool completely. Spread over chilled Coconut Layer.

To Decorate

3 tbsp	desiccated coconut
4	maraschino cherries, halved

Sprinkle coconut over pineapple layer and arrange cherries on top.

Serves 12.

HAUPIA

250 ml .	½ pt	water
75 gm .	3 oz	desiccated coconut
4½ tbsp .	5 tbsp	cornflour
2½ tbsp .	3 tbsp	sugar
250 ml .	½ pt	milk

Place water and coconut in liquidizer and blend on high speed for 45 seconds. Mix cornflour and sugar and gradually add cold milk. Add coconut mixture and mix well. Cook, stirring, over low heat, or in top of double saucepan, until thickened. Pour into square shallow baking tin and chill until firm. Cut into squares.

Serves 8 — 10.

MACADAMIA CHEESECAKE

Crust

70 gm .	2½ oz	plain flour
25 gm .	1 oz	sugar
25 gm .	1 oz	finely chopped Macadamia nuts or hazel nuts
40 gm .	1½ oz	butter, melted

Filling

	2	eggs, beaten
85 gm .	3 oz	sugar
	3 tbsp	milk
	3 tbsp	lemon juice
225 gm .	8 oz	cream cheese

Combine flour, sugar and nuts. Add melted butter and mix well. Press mixture into 9-in (23-cm) pie plate. Bake in a moderate oven (350°F, 180°C, Gas Mark 4) for 15 minutes. Cool 5 minutes. Combine ingredients for Filling and mix well. Pour into crust and bake another 30 minutes, or until set. Cool.

Serves 8.

HAWAIIAN SUNDAE

1 large	scoop vanilla ice cream
4 tbsp	crushed pineapple
	desiccated coconut
	maraschino cherry

Place ice cream in parfait glass or dessert dish. Top with pineapple, sprinkle with coconut and place cherry on top.

BANANA BREAD

100 gm	4 oz	butter or margarine
175 gm	7 oz	sugar
	2	eggs
200 gm	8 oz	mashed ripe bananas (3 small)
150 gm	6 oz	plain flour
50 gm	2 oz	oatmeal
	1 tsp	baking powder
	½ tsp	bicarbonate of soda
	½ tsp	salt
50 gm	2 oz	chopped nuts

Cream butter with sugar and beat in eggs, one at a time. Stir in mashed bananas. Combine flour with oatmeal, baking powder, bicarbonate of soda, and salt. Beat into first mixture. Stir in nuts. Pour mixture into a greased loaf tin and bake in a moderate oven (350°F, 180°C, Gas Mark 4) for 65 minutes. Cool overnight before slicing.

FRENCH TOAST, HAWAIIAN STYLE

	2	eggs
	dash	salt
70 ml	1 gill	milk
225 gm	8 oz	tinned pineapple chunks
	6 slices	white bread
	2 tbsp	butter
	1 tsp	cinnamon
	2 tbsp	sugar

Beat eggs with salt. Beat in milk and juice from pineapple. Heat butter. Dip bread into egg-milk mixture, allowing mixture to soak in for a few seconds. Fry bread slices in butter until well browned on both sides. Top each slice with several chunks of pineapple and sprinkle with mixture of cinnamon and sugar.

Serves 6.

KALUA

500 gm	1¼ lb	sugar
330 ml	⅔ pt	water
50 gm	2 oz	instant coffee powder
250 ml	½ pt	vodka
	½	vanilla pod

Boil sugar, water and coffee together. Cool. Add vodka and vanilla pod and pour into large jar or bottle. Cover and store for thirty days. Discard vanilla pod. Serve as an after-dinner liqueur.

CHI CHI

3 tbsp	rum
5 tbsp	pineapple juice
5 tbsp	coconut milk*
	crushed ice

Combine in a shaker and strain into a glass. (Traditionally served in a coconut shell, garnished with an orchid.)
*Substitute 5 tbsp milk + 2 tbsp desiccated coconut. Leave standing 1 hour. Strain.

MAI TAI

1 tbsp	light rum
1 tbsp	dark rum
1 tbsp	Demerara rum
½ tbsp	Curaçao
dash	Orgeat syrup
1 tbsp	lime juice
1 tbsp	lemon juice
5 tbsp	orange juice
5 tbsp	pineapple juice
	crushed ice
2 chunks	pineapple
1	maraschino cherry

Combine all ingredients except pineapple chunks and cherry. Shake well and strain into a glass. Garnish with pineapple and cherry.

SOUTH SEA ISLAND PUNCH

500 ml . 1 pt	orange juice
500 ml . 1 pt	pineapple juice
1 l. . 1 qt	ginger ale
250 ml . ½ pt	rum or vodka (optional)
	ice cubes
1	lemon, thinly sliced

Combine juices, ginger ale, rum or vodka, and ice cubes in a punch bowl. Float lemon slices on top.

About 18 servings.

Special Traditions from Special People

The people of America have come from the whole world. The lines dividing them into groups cut many ways, through religions, nationalities, and races. Over the centuries, many groups have been merged into the whole, as Scotsman has married Swede, and Italian has married German. Family traditions have become blended as a young wife whose Greek mother taught her to cook moussaka has learned to cook the Yorkshire pudding her husband enjoyed as a child.

The traditions of certain groups have survived the blending process. Among these are Pennsylvania Dutch and the Basques. Jewish customs of cooking survive, especially in homes where kosher kitchens are still maintained, and Shaker traditions have outlived their authors. This is especially true of food, for good recipes will survive as long as there are good cooks.

THE PENNSYLVANIA DUTCH

They were not really Dutch, but Deutsch, for they came from Germany in the seventeenth century, eventually settling in Pennsylvania. Most were Mennonites or Old Order Amish, sometimes referred to as the Plain People because of their simple clothing and lifestyle. Today, their descendants still run the neat farms with the hearts and flowers painted in bright colours on the barn doors. The Amish still shun modern conveniences and have no telephones, radios or televisions. They travel by horse and buggy instead of by car. And they still believe in farming as a way of life.

Farm appetites are big and so are farm meals, especially in the Pennsylvania Dutch country. Breakfast might include scrapple, ham, eggs, potatoes, and even pie. Dinner is traditionally served at midday and supper in the evening, and it is said that a really festive Pennsylvania Dutch meal always includes seven sweets and seven sours.

There is much of the German influence in Pennsylvania Dutch cooking, and sauerkraut and dumplings are as popular in Lancaster County as in Bavaria. But a Shoo-fly Pie is pure Pennsylvania Dutch.

STUFFED PORK CHOPS	4 large, very thick	pork chops
	1 small	cooking apple
	85 gm . 3 oz	soft breadcrumbs
	2 tbsp	raisins
	1 tbsp	sugar
	½ tsp	salt
	2 tbsp	butter or margarine, melted
	2 tbsp	minced onion
	4 tbsp	hot water
		salt, pepper

Cut along the fat edge of each pork chop, through to the bone, forming a pocket. Peel, core and chop the apple and combine it with crumbs, raisins, sugar and salt. Melt butter and fry onion until tender; combine with apple and breadcrumb mixture. Add water and mix well. Stuff the pork chops, sprinkle with salt and pepper, and lay them in an ovenproof dish. Bake in a moderate oven (350°F, 180°C, Gas Mark 4) for 40 minutes. Cover dish and bake 20 minutes longer.

HAM LOAF	*340 gm . 12 oz*	minced ham
	340 gm . 12 oz	minced pork
	85 gm . 3 oz	fine breadcrumbs
	200 ml . 1½ gills	milk
	2	eggs
	4 tbsp	minced onion
	½ stick	celery, finely chopped
	¼ tsp	mustard powder
	⅛ tsp	pepper

Combine all ingredients and mix thoroughly. Shape into a loaf and place in a baking tin or shallow ovenproof dish. Bake in a very moderate oven (325°F, 170°C, Gas Mark 3) for 1½ hours. Serve hot or cold.
    Serves 6.

CHICKEN PIE	*250 gm . 8-10 oz*	boneless cooked chicken, cubed
	3 tbsp	butter or margarine
	1	onion, chopped
	6 tbsp	plain flour
	550 ml . 1 pt	chicken broth
	100 gm . 4 oz	peas
		salt and pepper
		shortcrust pastry for single-crust pie

Melt butter and fry onion until tender. Stir in flour. Add broth and peas and cook, stirring, until thickened. Add chicken and salt and pepper to taste. Pour into an ovenproof dish. Prepare pastry and roll out to fit top of dish. Cut several slits in crust and place over the chicken. Bake in a hot oven (425°F, 220°C, Gas Mark 7) until lightly browned.

Serves 4.

Turkey Pie

Use cooked cubed turkey in place of chicken.

CHICKEN LOAF	85 gm . 3 oz	breadcrumbs
	165 ml . ⅓ pt	milk
	2	eggs, beaten
	2 tbsp	chopped parsley
	2 tbsp	minced celery
	2 tbsp	minced onion
	½ tsp	salt
	¼ tsp	pepper
	pinch	thyme
	340 gm . 12 oz	cooked boneless chicken, cubed

Mix breadcrumbs with milk. Add eggs, parsley, celery, onion, salt, pepper and thyme and mix well. Stir in chicken and turn into greased loaf tin. Bake in a moderate oven (375°F, 190°C, Gas Mark 5) for 30 minutes.

Serves 6.

Turkey Loaf

Use cooked turkey in place of chicken.

SWEET-SOUR	900 gm . 2 lb	red cabbage
RED CABBAGE	450 gm . 1 lb	cooking apples
	180 ml . ⅓ pt	water
	50 gm . 2 oz	brown sugar
	2 tsp	cornflour
	5 tbsp	vinegar
	1½ tsp	salt
	⅛ tsp	pepper

Shred cabbage and peel, core and chop apples. Combine in large saucepan with water, and simmer, covered, until tender (15-20 minutes). Combine brown sugar, cornflour, vinegar, salt and pepper and stir into cabbage mixture. Cook, stirring, until thickened.

Serves 6 — 8.

POTATO PANCAKES	675 gm . 1½ lb	potatoes
	1 small	onion, chopped
	2	eggs, beaten
	4 tbsp	flour
	1 tsp	salt
		fat or oil for frying

Peel and grate potatoes. Squeeze out liquid and combine with onion, eggs, flour and salt; mix well. Melt a small amount of fat or oil in a large frying pan and drop mixture by spoonfuls into hot fat, flattening into 4-in. (10-cm) cakes. Brown on both sides.

Serves 6 — 8.

HOT GERMAN POTATO SALAD	900 gm . 2 lb	medium-sized potatoes
	100 gm . 4 oz	streaky bacon, diced
	1 tbsp	plain flour
	5 tbsp . ½ gill	water
	140 ml . 1 gill	vinegar
	1 tsp	salt
	½ tsp	sugar
	⅛ tsp	pepper
	1	onion, chopped

Boil potatoes in skins until tender. Peel and dice. Fry bacon until crisp and drain on paper towels. Stir flour into bacon fat, add water, vinegar, salt, sugar and pepper and cook, stirring, until thick and bubbly. Combine with onion, bacon, and hot, diced potatoes, and toss lightly. Serve hot.

Serves 6 — 8.

RED BEET EGGS	hard-boiled eggs, shelled
	liquid from pickled beetroot

Immerse the eggs in the liquid until they become pink.

SWEET-SOUR	1 small	cucumber
CUCUMBERS	¼ tsp	salt
	8 tbsp	cream
	4 tsp	vinegar
	4 tsp	sugar

Peel cucumber and slice thinly. Mix salt, cream, vinegar and sugar and pour over cucumber. Chill 1 hour, stirring occasionally. Serve on lettuce.
  Serves 4.

CINNAMON		Basic Sweet Roll Dough recipe,
ROLLS		halved quantities (see p. 187)
	50 gm . 2 oz	butter, softened
	3 tsp	cinnamon
	75 gm . 3 oz	brown sugar
	50 gm . 2 oz	raisins

Roll dough into rectangle ¼ in. (6 mm) thick. Spread butter over dough and sprinkle evenly with cinnamon and brown sugar. Scatter raisins over and roll up dough from long side. Pinch seam closed and cut roll into 1-in (25-mm) slices. Arrange, cut side up, in greased baking tin or tins, leaving slight space between. Leave to rise in warm place until doubled. Bake in moderate oven (375°F, 190°C, Gas Mark 5) for 25-30 minutes. While warm, spread Glaze Icing (see p. 99) over the top.
  About 16 rolls.

RAISIN PIE		shortcrust pastry for
		double-crust pie
	200 gm . 8 oz	raisins
	250 ml . ½ pt	water
	150 gm . 6 oz	brown sugar
	2 tbsp	cornflour
	6 tbsp . 5 tbsp	cold water
	1	lemon (rind and juice)

Prepare pastry and use half to line a 9-in. (23-cm) pie plate. Roll remainder into a circle for top crust. Combine raisins and water and heat to boiling. Simmer slowly 10 minutes. Add the sugar. Blend cornflour with cold water and stir into the raisin mixture. Cook over low heat, stirring, until thickened. Add lemon rind and juice and cool. Pour into pastry-lined plate and cover with top crust. Seal and crimp edges and prick top with fork. Bake in a hot oven (425°F, 220°C, Gas Mark 7) until lightly browned (about 20 minutes).

SHOO-FLY PIE

		shortcrust pastry for single-crust pie
140 ml	1 gill	treacle
140 ml	1 gill	boiling water
	¾ tsp	bicarbonate of soda
170 gm	6 oz	plain flour
85 gm	3 oz	granulated sugar
115 gm	4 oz	brown sugar
	1 tsp	baking powder
	2 tbsp	cooking fat

Prepare pastry and line 9-in. (23-cm) pie plate. Combine treacle and boiling water and mix well. Stir in soda. Cool. Mix flour, sugars and baking powder and rub in fat until crumbly. Spread half of crumbs in pastry and pour half of treacle mixture over. Repeat. Bake in hot oven (425°F, 220°C, Gas Mark 7) for 10 minutes. Reduce heat (325°F, 170°C, Gas Mark 3) and bake until set (25-35 minutes).

BLACK BOTTOM PIE

		shortcrust pastry for single-crust pie, baked or Crumb Crust (see p. 173)
	1½ tbsp	cornflour
	¼ tsp	salt
100 gm	4 oz	sugar
	3	egg yolks
400 ml	¾ pt	milk
	1 tbsp	unflavoured gelatine
	5 tbsp	milk
40 gm	1½ oz	semi-sweet chocolate, melted
	1 tsp	vanilla essence
	3	egg whites
100 gm	3 oz	sugar
275 ml	½ pt	heavy cream
	2 tbsp	sugar
		grated chocolate

Prepare and bake pastry in 9-in (23-cm) pie plate. Blend cornflour, salt, sugar. Mix egg yolks with milk and stir into cornflour mixture. Cook over medium heat, stirring, until mixture boils. Stir gelatine into 5 tablespoons milk to soften. Add *half* of the custard mixture and stir until blended. Chill until thick but not set. Add melted chocolate and vanilla to remaining custard and mix well. Pour into pastry crust. Beat egg whites until stiff and continue beating while adding sugar, 1 tablespoon at a time. Fold into chilled gelatine-custard mixture and spread over chocolate mixture. Beat cream with 2 tablespoons sugar and spread over top. Garnish with grated chocolate.

APPLESAUCE CAKE

100 gm	4 oz	butter or margarine
200 gm	8 oz	brown sugar
	2	eggs
375 ml	¾ pt	applesauce
200 gm	8 oz	plain flour
	1 tsp	bicarbonate of soda
	½ tsp	cinnamon
	¼ tsp	cloves
	½ tsp	nutmeg
	¾ tsp	ginger
100 gm	4 oz	raisins

Cream butter and sugar. Beat in eggs, then applesauce. Mix flour with bicarbonate of soda and spices. Add to applesauce mixture and beat well. Blend in raisins. Pour into buttered cake tin or loaf tin and bake in a moderate oven (350°F, 180°C, Gas Mark 4) for 75 minutes. Remove from pan immediately and cool. Ice top and sides with Cream Cheese Frosting.

CREAM CHEESE FROSTING

100 gm	4 oz	cream cheese
3 tbsp	1½ oz	butter
200 gm	8 oz	icing sugar

Allow cream cheese and butter to soften at room temperature. Blend well. Gradually add icing sugar to cheese mixture and beat until very smooth.

APPLE BUTTER

2 l.	4 pt	apple juice
3 kg	8 lb	cooking apples
1 kg	2½ lb	sugar
2½ tsp	3 tsp	cinnamon

Peel, core and quarter apples. Place in large saucepan and pour cider over them. Simmer gently until very soft. Add sugar and cinnamon and stir until sugar dissolves. Continue cooking, stirring frequently, until very thick and a rich brown colour. Spoon into hot sterilized jars and seal.

THE SHAKERS

In the eighteenth century, a group of people sailed from England to America and established in New England a religious sect known as the Shakers. The name derived from the fact that intense religious fervour generated during worship services caused the participants to shake. These people lived in farming communes where all shared equally both labour and rewards. Eventually, the sect spread to other areas, including Shakertown, Kentucky, now called Pleasant Hill and preserved as a tourist attraction.

Since Shakers did not believe in marriage or in producing children, and since conversions eventually began to decline, the sect dwindled. However, many Shaker traditions have survived. Their expertly crafted furniture is highly prized, and many of their recipes continue to be a part of American culinary tradition.

SHAKER	*450 gm* . 1 lb	boneless cooked chicken
CHICKEN	4 tbsp	butter or margarine
PUDDING	1 small	onion, chopped
	1 stick	celery, chopped
	1	cooking apple, peeled and diced
	4 tbsp	flour
	140 ml . 1 gill	chicken broth
	275 ml . ½ pt	cream or milk
	1 tsp	salt
	⅛ tsp	pepper
	¼ tsp	nutmeg
Topping	*100 gm* . 4 oz	breadcrumbs
	2 tbsp	butter, melted

Melt butter, add onion, celery and apple, and fry until tender. Stir in flour and add broth, cream and seasonings. Cook, stirring, until thickened. Stir in chicken and turn into an ovenproof dish. Mix breadcrumbs with melted butter and spread over top. Bake in a very moderate oven (325°F, 170°C, Gas Mark 3) for 30 minutes.

Serves 4 — 6.

CHOCOLATE	*500 ml* . 1 pt	milk
BREAD PUDDING	*50 gm* . 2 oz	semi-sweet chocolate
	75 gm . 3 oz	soft bread cubes
	50 gm . 2 oz	sugar
	50 gm . 2 oz	chopped nuts
	2	eggs, beaten

Heat milk, chocolate and sugar together in top of double saucepan, stirring until smooth. Stir in bread cubes, nuts and beaten eggs and mix well. Pour into greased ovenproof dish and place dish in baking tin of hot water. Bake in a moderate oven (350°F, 180°C, Gas Mark 4) until set (about 30 minutes). Serve warm with cream.

Serves 6.

STUFFED ONIONS	4 large	onions
	115 gm . 4 oz	minced cooked beef
	340 gm . 12 oz	spinach, cooked and well-drained
	50 gm . 2 oz	breadcrumbs
	¼ tsp	salt
	dash	pepper
	140 ml . 1 gill	beef stock

Peel onions and cook in boiling water 15 minutes. Remove centres, leaving thick shell. Combine beef, chopped spinach, crumbs, salt and pepper and stuff into onions. Place in an ovenproof dish and pour broth around them. Bake in a moderate oven (375°F, 190°C, Gas Mark 5) for 30 minutes.

Serves 4.

SUGAR PIE		shortcrust pastry for single-crust pie
	50 gm . 2 oz	butter
	200 gm . 8 oz	brown sugar
	4½ tbsp . 5 tbsp	plain flour
	500 ml . 1 pt	thick cream
	½ tsp	vanilla essence
		nutmeg

Prepare pastry and line a 9-in. (23-cm) pie plate. Mix butter, brown sugar and flour and stir in cream and vanilla. Pour into crust, sprinkle with nutmeg, and bake in a hot oven (450°F, 230°C, Gas Mark 8) for 10 minutes. Reduce heat (350°F, 180°C, Gas Mark 4) and bake until set.

RHUBARB CUSTARD PIE		shortcrust pastry for single-crust pie
	225 gm . 8 oz	chopped rhubarb
	2½ tsp	cornflour
	280 gm . 10 oz	sugar
	2	egg yolks
	275 ml . ½ pt	milk

Prepare pastry and line a 9-in. (23-cm) pie plate. Place rhubarb in the pastry. Mix cornflour, sugar and egg yolks and stir in milk. Mix well and pour over rhubarb. Bake in a hot oven (450°F, 230°C, Gas Mark 8) for 10 minutes. Reduce heat (350°F, 180°C, Gas Mark 4) and bake until filling is set and rhubarb is soft (about 30 minutes). Cool and serve with whipped cream.

APPLE CIDER			
APPLE CIDER CAKE	150 gm . 6 oz	butter or margarine
	400 gm . 1 lb	sugar
	3	eggs
	400 gm . 1 lb	plain flour
	¾ tsp	bicarbonate of soda
	½ tsp	salt
	1¼ tsp . 1½ tsp	nutmeg
	125 ml . 1 gill	apple juice or sweet cider

Cream butter and sugar. Beat in eggs. Sieve flour, soda, salt and nutmeg together and add to creamed mixture alternately with cider. Pour into well-greased cake or loaf tin and bake in a moderate oven (350°F, 180°C, Gas Mark 4) for 75-90 minutes.

THE BASQUES: HERDING SHEEP IN A NEW LAND

The settling of the American West opened up thousands of acres of grazing land. For large flocks of sheep ranging for months at a time far from the nearest town, experienced shepherds were necessary. A responsible shepherd would be aware of the dangers of wild animals and would know where watering holes could be found in his area. Above all, he would understand the ways of his sheep.

The Basque shepherds were ideal for the situation. For centuries their ancestors had herded sheep in the Pyrenees of France and Spain, passing their knowledge from father to son. Thousands of these Basques travelled to remote areas of the West. Most of them went on a temporary basis, working under contract, but few returned home. They settled in the areas where they had worked, and many bought their own land and sheep.

There is not much open grazing today, but the Basques remain, living in small towns in Nevada, Idaho and Southeastern Oregon. Some have moved further from the land, and there is a community of several thousand Basques in Boise, capital city of Idaho.

Basque cooking is neither French nor Spanish, but reminiscent of both, often using tomatoes, green peppers, onions and garlic. Not surprisingly, lamb is a basic ingredient in many recipes.

BASQUE LAMB STEW		
	1 tbsp	butter
900 gm .	2 lb	lean lamb cubes
	1	onion, chopped
	1 clove	garlic, crushed
	3 tbsp	plain flour
	1 tsp	salt
	¼ tsp	pepper
550 ml .	1 pt	water
	4	carrots, peeled and sliced
	1	green pepper, chopped
	2	tomatoes, chopped
	2 sticks	celery, sliced
	2 large	potatoes, diced

Melt butter and brown lamb with onion and garlic. Stir in flour, salt and pepper, and add water gradually. Add carrots, green pepper, tomatoes and celery and simmer 1½ hours, stirring frequently, adding water if necessary. Add potatoes and simmer 30 minutes.
   Serves 6.

LAMB LOAF		
	2	eggs, beaten
200 ml .	1½ gills	milk
85 gm .	3 oz	soft breadcrumbs
675 gm .	1½ lb	raw minced lamb
	¼	onion, chopped
	½	green pepper, chopped
	2 tbsp	chopped parsley
	1 tsp	salt
	¼ tsp	pepper

Mix eggs, milk and crumbs and leave to stand 10 minutes. Add remaining ingredients and mix well. Pack into a loaf pan or shape into a loaf and place in a baking tin. Bake in a moderate oven (350°F, 180°C, Gas Mark 4) for 1 hour. Serve with Tomato Sauce or Parsley Sauce (see p. 157).
   Serves 4 — 6.

LAMB WITH	**CHICKPEAS**		

LAMB WITH	450 gm . 1 lb	minced raw lamb
CHICKPEAS	1	onion, chopped
	2 cloves	garlic, crushed
	1 tbsp	butter or margarine
	450 gm . 1 lb	tinned chickpeas, with liquid
	100 gm . 4 oz	white rice
	325 ml . ⅔ pt	water
	½ tsp	salt
	¼ tsp	pepper

Fry lamb, onion and garlic in the butter until brown. Combine with remaining ingredients and pour into an ovenproof dish. Cover and bake in a very moderate oven (325°F, 170°C, Gas Mark 3) for 1 hour.
  Serves 4.

BASQUE BEEF	1 tbsp	cooking oil
AND RICE	675 gm . 1½ lb	stewing beef, cubed
	1	onion, coarsely chopped
	1 clove	garlic, crushed
	3 tbsp	plain flour
	1 tsp	salt
	¼ tsp	pepper
	3	tomatoes, chopped
	800 ml . 1½ pt	water
	100 gm . 4 oz	white rice

Heat oil and brown beef, onion and garlic. Stir in flour and add salt, pepper, tomatoes and water. Cover and simmer gently 1½ hours, stirring occasionally. Add rice and continue cooking 20 minutes or until rice is tender.
  Serves 6.

BASQUE ROAST	2½ kg . 5-6 lb	roasting hen, oven-ready
CHICKEN		giblets (liver, heart, gizzard)
	140 gm . 5 oz	white rice
	1	onion, chopped
	1 stick	celery, diced
	½ tsp	sage
	⅛ tsp	pepper
	½ tsp	salt
	4 tbsp	butter or margarine

Simmer giblets in water until tender; drain, saving liquid. Place rice, onion and celery in saucepan with 3 pt (1½ l.) cold water. Bring to boil and simmer 10 minutes; drain. Chop giblets and combine with hot rice, seasonings and butter and mix well. Spoon into cavities of chicken. Pull skin flap over neck cavity and fasten with skewer or toothpicks. Close body cavity by pushing three or four poultry skewers through and lacing with twine. Tie the twine around the legs of the bird then around the body and tie ends. Roast, uncovered, in a very moderate oven (325°F, 170°C, Gas Mark 3) until tender (3-3½ hours). Serve with Chicken Gravy.

Chicken Gravy

Pour off all but 3 tablespoons of drippings in roasting pan and stir in 3 tablespoons flour. Add water to liquid in which giblets were cooked, sufficient to make 1 pt (550 ml) and add gradually to mixture in pan. Add ½ teaspoon salt and ⅛ teaspoon pepper. Cook, stirring, until thickened.

BASQUE	*450 gm* . 1 lb	cod fillets
CODFISH		flour, salt, pepper
	4 tbsp	cooking oil
	1 small	onion, chopped
	1 clove	garlic, crushed
	2 tbsp	flour
	275 ml . ½ pt	milk
	¼ tsp	salt
	dash	pepper
	2 tbsp	chopped parsley

Flour cod fillets, sprinkle with salt and pepper and fry in hot oil until brown on both sides. Remove fish to a greased ovenproof dish. Add onion and garlic to the oil in frying pan and fry until tender. Stir in flour and gradually add milk. Add salt and pepper and cook until thickened. Pour over fish and sprinkle with parsley. Bake in a moderate oven (350°F, 180°C, Gas Mark 4) for 30 minutes.
  Serves 4.

BASQUE	*115 gm* . 4 oz	sausages
OMELETTE	8	eggs
	½ tsp	salt
	¼ tsp	pepper

Slice the sausages and fry until brown. Beat eggs with salt and pepper and pour over sausages. Cook on very low heat, without stirring, until set.
Serves 4 — 6.

MUSHROOM   *115 gm* . 4 oz   sliced mushrooms
OMELETTE   1 clove   garlic, crushed
                         2 tbsp   butter
                              6   eggs
                          ½ tsp   salt
                          ⅛ tsp   pepper
                         1 tbsp   chopped parsley

Fry mushrooms and garlic in butter until tender. Beat eggs with salt, pepper and parsley and pour over the mushrooms. Cook on low heat, without stirring, until set.
Serves 4.

BASQUE   ·4   medium potatoes, peeled
POTATOES AND   and sliced
EGGS   4 tbsp   fat
                              4   eggs, beaten
                          ½ tsp   salt
                          ¼ tsp   pepper
                          1 tsp   chopped spring onion
                         2 tbsp   chopped parsley
                          ¼ tsp   thyme

Fry potatoes in fat until tender and lightly browned. Mix eggs with remaining ingredients and pour over potatoes. Cook over low heat, without stirring, until eggs are set.
Serves 4.

SHEEPHERDER   *150 gm* . 6 oz   dried red kidney beans
BEANS   *50 gm* . 2 oz   bacon, chopped
                              1   onion, chopped
                          1 tsp   salt
                          ¼ tsp   pepper

Soak beans overnight; drain. Put beans in a large saucepan and cover completely with fresh water. Simmer until tender (about 1 hour). Fry bacon with onion and add to beans with salt and pepper. Simmer, covered, 45 minutes.

POTATO	450 gm . 1 lb	potatoes
CASSEROLE	4 tbsp	butter
	½	onion, minced
	1 clove	garlic, crushed
	2 tbsp	plain flour
	400 ml . ¾ pt	milk
	1 tsp	salt
	⅛ tsp	pepper
	2 tbsp	chopped parsley

Peel potatoes and cut into thick slices. Place in greased ovenproof dish. Fry onion and garlic in butter until tender. Stir in flour and add milk and seasonings. Cook until thickened and pour over potatoes. Cover and bake in a moderate oven (325°F, 170°C, Gas Mark 3) until tender (45-60 minutes).

Serves 4 — 6.

FRIED GREEN	2 rashers	streaky bacon, chopped
PEPPERS	6	green peppers
	1 small	onion, thinly sliced
	1 clove	garlic, crushed
	½ tsp	salt

Fry bacon 5 minutes. Remove seeds from peppers and cut into strips. Add to bacon with onion, garlic and salt and continue cooking, stirring frequently, until tender.

Serves 4 — 6.

RICE PANCAKES	200 gm . 7 oz	cooked white rice
	2	eggs
	275 ml . ½ pt	milk
	140 gm . 5 oz	plain flour
	2 tsp	baking powder
	½ tsp	salt
	2 tbsp	melted butter

Mix rice with eggs. Add milk gradually. Mix flour, baking powder and salt and add to rice mixture. Add melted butter and stir until blended. Drop by heaped spoonfuls onto hot griddle and cook on medium heat until bottom is brown and top begins to look dry. Turn and brown other side. Serve hot with butter and honey or syrup.

Serves 4.

OATMEAL PIE

		shortcrust pastry for single-crust pie
50 gm	2 oz	quick-cooking oatmeal
40 gm	1½ oz	desiccated coconut
150 gm	6 oz	sugar
	pinch	salt
125 ml	1 gill	milk
	2	eggs, beaten
50 gm	2 oz	butter, melted
165 ml	⅓ pt	dark corn syrup
	½ tsp	vanilla essence

Prepare pastry and line 9-in. (23-cm) pie plate. Mix oatmeal, coconut, sugar and salt and spread over pastry. Combine milk, eggs, melted butter, syrup and vanilla and mix well. Pour over oatmeal mixture and bake in a hot oven (450°F, 230°C, Gas Mark 8) for 10 minutes. Reduce heat (350°F, 180°C, Gas Mark 4) and bake 30 minutes or until set. Serve plain or with whipped cream.

A JEWISH HANUKKAH BRUNCH

Hanukkah is the Jewish Feast of Lights, an eight-day festival which usually falls in the month of December. Families celebrate in their homes, observing the ancient prayers and traditions. An extra candle in the Hanukkah *menorah* is lit each evening until all eight candles are alight. Gifts are exchanged and special games are played by children.

In some American towns and cities, Jewish women have sponsored community celebrations of the feast. Their Hanukkah Brunch is a sellout occasion, attended by people of all religions. The queues are long but the food is worth waiting for. There are *bagels* (a kind of roll) spread with cream cheese and *lox* (smoked salmon); cheese blintzes with sour cream and strawberry preserves; poppy-seed cakes and carrot cakes; and plenty of hot coffee.

Undoubtedly bagels and blintzes are common in Jewish homes in many countries, but where but in the United States could one find a community Hanukkah Brunch?

CHEESE BLINTZES			
		3	eggs, beaten
	200 ml	1½ gills	milk
		2 tbsp	salad oil
		½ tsp	salt
		2 tbsp	water
	85 gm	3 oz	plain flour
			Cheese Filling
			sour cream
			jam or preserves

Add milk, oil, salt and water to beaten eggs. Beat in flour. Heat a small lightly greased frying pan and pour in 3 tablespoons of batter. Cook on one side only until top is dry and bottom is browned. Turn out onto a clean cloth, brown side up. Place 1 heaped tablespoonful of Cheese Filling in centre of each blintz and fold four sides over filling. Place, seam side down, in a buttered baking tin, brush with melted butter, and bake in a moderately hot oven (400°F, 200°C, Gas Mark 6) until brown. Serve hot, with sour cream and jam.

Approximately 18 Blintzes.

Cheese Filling	*450 gm* . 1 lb	cottage cheese, pressed through a sieve
	1	egg yolk
	3 tbsp	sugar
	¼ tsp	cinnamon
	¼ tsp	salt

Mix well and use as filling for Blintzes.

CARROT CAKE	*165 ml* . ⅓ pt	salad oil
	225 gm . 9 oz	sugar
	2	egg yolks
	2 tbsp. .2½ tbsp	hot water
	125 gm . 5 oz	plain flour
	¾ tsp	baking powder
	¼ tsp	bicarbonate of soda
	½ tsp	nutmeg
	½ tsp	cinnamon
	½ tsp	ginger
	⅛ tsp	salt
	50 gm . 2 oz	chopped nuts
	150 gm . 6 oz	grated carrots
	2	egg whites

Beat oil, sugar and egg yolks together thoroughly. Add hot water and mix well. Sieve flour, baking powder, bicarbonate of soda, spices and salt and add to mixture. Beat well. Stir in carrots and nuts. Beat egg whites until stiff and fold in. Turn into greased loaf tin and bake in moderate oven (375°F, 190°C, Gas Mark 5) for 40-45 minutes.

POPPY SEED	75 gm . 3 oz	butter or margarine
CAKE	200 gm . 8 oz	sugar
	2	egg yolks
	1	egg white
	¾ tsp	vanilla essence
	200 gm . 8 oz	plain flour
	2½ tsp . 3 tsp	baking powder
	¼ tsp	salt
	165 ml . ⅓ pt	milk
	5 tsp . 2 tbsp	poppy seeds

Cream butter and sugar together. Beat in eggs and vanilla. Sieve flour, baking powder and salt together and add to creamed mixture alternately with milk. Beat until well blended. Fold in poppy seeds. Turn into greased 9-in. (23-cm) square baking tin and bake in a moderate oven (350°F, 180°C, Gas Mark 4) for 25-30 minutes.

BAGELS AND	4	bagels, split and toasted
LOX	115 gm . 4 oz	cream cheese
	115 gm . 4 oz	smoked salmon

Spread both halves of each bagel with cream cheese and put together with salmon between. OR blend the cream cheese and salmon together and spread mixture on bagel halves.

CHICKEN SOUP	2½ kg . 5-6 lb	chicken, quartered
	3 l. . 2½ qt	water
	1	onion, chopped
	1	carrot, chopped
	2 sticks	celery, chopped
	4 tbsp	chopped parsley
	1 tbsp	salt
	¼ tsp	pepper

Place all ingredients in large saucepan and simmer, covered, until meat falls from bones. Strain. Chill several hours until fat rises and solidifies. Remove fat. Re-heat broth and add noodles or dumplings. Simmer until cooked.

6 — 8 servings.

Note: Chicken may be boned and skinned after cooking and used in any recipe requiring cooked chicken.

CHOPPED CHICKEN LIVERS

900 gm .	2 lb	chicken livers
	1	onion
	2 tbsp	salad oil
	3	eggs, hard-boiled
	1 tsp	salt
	⅛ tsp	pepper

Fry liver and onion in oil until tender. Cool. Mince liver, onion and eggs together and mix well with salt and pepper. Add a little more oil if necessary to bind mixture together. Serve on crackers.

LATKES

450 gm .	1 lb	potatoes
	2 tbsp	flour
	¾ tsp	salt
	⅛ tsp	pepper
	2	eggs, beaten
		fat for frying

Peel and grate potatoes. Place in strainer and press out liquid. Add flour, salt, pepper and eggs. Mix well. Heat small amount of fat in large frying pan and drop batter by tablespoonfuls, spreading into 4-in. (10-cm) cakes. Cook over medium heat until well browned on both sides. Serve with Applesauce.

APPLESAUCE

1 kg .	2 lb	cooking apples
200 gm .	6 oz	sugar
	½ tsp	cinnamon
		water

Peel, core and chop the apples and place them in a large saucepan. Add water to barely cover. Simmer, stirring frequently, until soft (about 1 hour). Add sugar and cinnamon and cook 30 minutes, stirring frequently.

TZIMMES

400 gm .	1 lb	carrots, sliced
50 gm .	2 oz	butter
125 ml .	1 gill	orange juice
3½ tbsp .	4 tbsp	honey or brown sugar
	½ tsp	salt
	1 tbsp	chopped parsley

Fry carrots gently in butter, stirring frequently, for 10 minutes. Add orange juice, salt and honey and mix well. Cover pan and simmer 1 hour. Sprinkle with parsley.
Serves 6.

SPICED BEETS

2 large	beetroots, cooked
1	onion, thinly sliced
5 tbsp	vinegar
¼ tsp	salt
⅛ tsp	pepper
⅛ tsp	cinnamon
2 tsp	brown sugar

Peel and slice beetroots and place layers of beetroot and onion in a shallow dish. Combine vinegar, salt, pepper, cinnamon and brown sugar and bring to boil. Simmer 2 minutes. Pour over vegetables, cover dish and chill several hours.

Serves 3 — 4.

Christmas in the United States

A COLLAGE OF CUSTOMS

Christmas in twentieth-century America is the brightest holiday of the year: a season of warmth and light in the middle of the coldness and darkness of winter. In churches, stars shine down on mangers, and Advent candles glow on altars. Lighted decorations arc over downtown streets, and coloured lights brighten the eaves of houses and twinkle on the shrubbery. Groups of carollers go from door to door singing *Joy to the World* and orchestras and choirs present Handel's *Messiah* in concert. Tchaikovsky's *Nutcracker* ballet is danced on stages across the country. The Christmas stories of Charles Dickens come to life on television screens.

Inside the homes, pine boughs and holly are woven into garlands, and fat red and green candles scent the air with frangipani and bayberry. Christmas trees are decorated with coloured lights and ornaments of glass and felt, collected year by year and often handmade. Small children mark off the days on Advent calendars and hang red felt stockings by fireplaces. Young people kiss beneath the mistletoe. Each day, the display of Christmas cards grows larger.

The customs, like the people, have come from around the world. Some, like the old English carols, came over on the *Mayflower*, but the Christmas card had not then been invented and Dickens had not been born. Each new wave of immigrants brought a new set of traditions. From Germany has come the Christmas tree, while Scandinavians have brought the Julebord and the custom of choosing a Lucia bride to wear a crown of candles. Children of Mexican descent gather at parties to break the piñatas with sticks, releasing a shower of sweets and gifts. But it was an American-born clergyman, Clement Moore, who wrote the poem *'Twas the Night Before Christmas* and spread the image of a red-suited Santa Claus across the world.

The multi traditions are especially evident in the kitchens as the aroma of fruits and spices, of chocolate and anise and brandy, drifts through the houses in the weeks preceding Christmas, a tantalizing forerunner of Christmas feasting.

CHRISTMAS STOLLEN

Basic Sweet Roll Dough
   recipe - halve quantities
   (see p. 187)

40 gm . 1½ oz	raisins
30 gm . 1 oz	chopped candied peel
25 gm . 1 oz	halved candied cherries
2 tbsp	butter, melted
	White Glaze Icing

Knead the dough, adding raisins a few at a time and working them into it. Add peel in same way, and continue to knead until fruit is evenly distributed throughout the dough. Place in a clean, greased basin, turning to grease all surfaces. Cover with a cloth and put in a warm place to rise until doubled (about 1 hour). Punch down dough and flatten into an oval. Brush with melted butter and fold in half lengthwise. Brush top with remaining melted butter and place on a greased baking sheet. Place again in a warm place until doubled (45-60 minutes). Bake in a moderate oven (350°F, 180°C, Gas Mark 4) for 30 minutes, or until lightly browned. While warm, spread White Glaze Icing over the top and decorate with candied cherries.

White Glaze Icing

85 gm . 3 oz	icing sugar
2 tsp	milk

Mix until very smooth.

DARK FRUITCAKE

400 gm . 1 lb	mixed candied peels
100 gm . 4 oz	chopped nuts
100 gm . 4 oz	raisins
100 gm . 4 oz	currants
3½ tbsp . 4 tbsp	sherry
3½ tbsp . 4 tbsp	orange juice
5 tsp . 2 tbsp	brandy
3½ tbsp . 4 tbsp	treacle
1 tsp	cinnamon
1 tsp	nutmeg
½ tsp . 1 tsp	cloves
1 tsp	ginger
150 gm . 6 oz	plain flour
½ tsp	salt
¼ tsp	bicarbonate of soda
100 gm . 4 oz	butter or margarine
150 gm . 6 oz	brown sugar
3	eggs

Combine fruits, nuts, treacle and liquids and mix well. Sieve spices with flour, salt and soda. Cream butter with sugar. Beat in eggs one at a time. Stir in flour mixture. Fold in fruit and mix well. Butter a large loaf tin and line with heavy paper. Butter the inside of the paper and turn the batter into it. Bake in a slow oven (300°F, 150°C, Gas Mark 2) for 1½-2 hours. Cool. Remove paper and rewrap in foil. Will keep several weeks.

SOUTHERN WHITE FRUITCAKE

200 gm .	8 oz	butter
200 gm .	8 oz	sugar
medium .	6 large	eggs
1 tsp .	1½ tsp	cinnamon
	1 tsp	nutmeg
	½ tsp	ginger
250 gm .	10 oz	plain flour
1 tsp .	1¼ tsp	baking powder
	¾ tsp	salt
125 ml .	1 gill	sherry
100 gm .	4 oz	desiccated coconut
75 gm .	3 oz	chopped nuts
400 gm .	1 lb	sultanas
150 gm .	6 oz	raisins
300 gm .	12 oz	chopped peel

Cream butter and sugar thoroughly. Beat in eggs singly. Sieve spices with flour, baking powder and salt. Add half of dry mixture to batter. Add sherry and mix well. Add remaining flour mixture. Fold in coconut, nuts and fruits and mix thoroughly. Pour batter into well-greased large cake tin and bake in a slow oven (300°F, 150°C, Gas Mark 2) for approximately 2 hours.

RUM BALLS

150 gm .	6 oz	sweetmeal biscuits, crushed
100 gm .	4 oz	nuts, finely chopped
2½ tbsp .	3 tbsp	corn syrup or golden syrup
5 tsp .	2 tbsp	rum
100 gm .	4 oz	icing sugar
		additional icing sugar for coating

Combine all ingredients and mix thoroughly. Shape into 1-in. (25-mm) balls and roll in icing sugar. Store in covered container.

Brandy Balls

Use brandy in place of rum in above recipe.

GINGERBREAD	200 gm . 8 oz	butter or margarine
COOKIES	200 gm . 8 oz	brown sugar
	125 ml . 1 gill	treacle
	400 gm . 1 lb	plain flour
	1 tsp	bicarbonate of soda
	1 tsp	salt
	2½ tsp . 1 tbsp	ginger

Cream butter and sugar together; add treacle and mix well. Combine flour, soda, salt and ginger and stir into first mixture. Chill. Roll out onto lightly floured board to ¼-in. (6-mm) thickness and cut into shapes with biscuit cutters. Place on ungreased baking sheet and bake in a moderate oven (375°F, 190°C, Gas Mark 5) for 10-12 minutes.

About 3 dozen.

MINCEMEAT	100 gm . 4 oz	butter or margarine
COOKIES	100 gm . 4 oz	brown sugar
	1	egg
	150 gm . 6 oz	mincemeat
	1¾ tsp . 2 tsp	lemon juice
	200 gm . 8 oz	plain flour
	½ tsp	bicarbonate of soda
	½ tsp	salt

Cream butter and sugar together and beat in egg. Add mincemeat and lemon juice. Sieve flour with soda and salt and stir into mincemeat mixture. Drop by teaspoonfuls onto buttered baking sheet 2 in. (5 cm) apart and bake in a moderate oven (375°F, 190°C, Gas Mark 5) for 10 minutes.

3-4 dozen cookies.

SHORTBREAD	200 gm . 8 oz	plain flour
SQUARES	¼ tsp	baking powder
	¼ tsp	salt
	50 gm . 2 oz	icing sugar
	200 gm . 8 oz	butter

Mix flour, baking powder, salt and sugar. Cut in butter with pastry blender or two knives. Turn into ungreased 9-in. (23-cm) square baking tin and press down *firmly* and evenly. Bake in a moderate oven (350°F, 180°C, Gas Mark 4) for 25 minutes. Cut into squares while warm.

MEXICAN	200 gm . 8 oz	butter or margarine
WEDDING CAKES	100 gm . 4 oz	icing sugar
	1 tsp	vanilla essence
	250 gm . 10 oz	plain flour
	¼ tsp	salt
	75 gm . 3 oz	nuts, finely chopped
		icing sugar for coating

Cream butter with sugar and vanilla. Mix flour, salt and nuts and stir into creamed mixture. Shape into 1-in. (25-mm) balls and place on ungreased baking sheet. Bake in a moderately hot oven (400°F, 200°C, Gas Mark 6) until set (10-12 minutes). Roll in icing sugar, cool, and roll again in icing sugar.

4 dozen.

DATE-NUT	125 gm . 5 oz	chopped dates
BREAD	75 gm . 3 oz	chopped nuts
	½ tsp	salt
	1¼ tsp . 1½ tsp	bicarbonate of soda
	2½ tsp . 3 tbsp	butter or margarine
	165 ml . ⅓ pt	boiling water
	2	eggs, beaten
	1 tsp	vanilla essence
	150 gm . 6 oz	plain flour
	150 g, . 6 oz	sugar

Mix dates, nuts, salt and soda. Add butter and boiling water and mix well. Stir in eggs and vanilla. Sieve flour with sugar and add to mixture. Turn into greased loaf tin and bake in a moderate oven (350°F, 180°C, Gas Mark 4) for 60-70 minutes. Cool 10 minutes. Remove from pan and cool several hours before slicing.

NESSELRODE	1½ tbsp	unflavoured gelatine
	250 ml . ½ pt	milk
	6 medium . 6 large	egg yolks
	125 gm . 5 oz	sugar
	125 ml . 1 gill	sherry
	½ tsp	almond essence
	190 ml . 1½ gills	thick cream
	6 medium . 6 large	egg whites
	75 gm . 3 oz	chopped mixed peel
	25 gm . 1 oz	chopped candied cherries
		whipped cream and cherries for decorating

Sprinkle gelatine over milk and heat until dissolved. Beat egg yolks until thick and beat in sugar gradually. Add milk-gelatine mixture, sherry and almond essence and mix well. Chill until syrupy but *do not allow to set*. Beat cream until stiff and fold into chilled mixture. Beat egg whites and fold in. Fold in peel and cherries and pour into large glass dish. Chill several hours or overnight. Decorate with whipped cream and cherries.

Serves 8.

AMBROSIA

	6	large oranges
100 gm .	4 oz	desiccated coconut
75 gm .	3 oz	sugar
	6	maraschino cherries

Peel oranges and divide into segments, removing all pith, membranes and seeds. Layer one-third of the oranges in a glass dish, and sprinkle with one-third of the sugar and one-third of the coconut. Repeat twice more. Decorate with cherries. Cover and chill several hours.

Serves 8.

CHRISTMAS FRUIT SALAD

	1 packet	lime jelly
	1 packet	cherry jelly
900 gm .	2 lb	tinned fruit cocktail, well-drained
	2	bananas, sliced
100 gm .	4 oz	miniature marshmallows
400 ml .	¾ pt	thick cream, whipped

Prepare lime jelly, using only *half* usual amount of water. Pour into shallow dish and chill until very firm. Prepare cherry jelly in same way. Cut into cubes. Mix fruit cocktail with bananas and marshmallows. Fold in whipped cream. Add the cubed jelly and turn into a large glass bowl.

Serves 12.

STUFFED PRUNES

	2 dozen	large dried prunes
75 gm .	3 oz	cream cheese
4 tsp .	1½ tbsp	butter
100 gm .	4 oz	icing sugar

Slit prunes along one side and remove stones. Mix cream cheese and butter until well blended. Gradually blend in icing sugar, beating until smooth. Stuff prunes with the cream cheese mixture.

Stuffed Dates

Use 3 dozen dates in place of prunes in above recipe.

CHRISTMAS CONSERVE			
1 kg	.	2½ lb	oranges
200 gm	.	8 oz	lemons
1½ kg	.	3½ lb	sugar
1 l.	.	2 pt	water
50 gm	.	2 oz	nuts, finely chopped
100 gm	.	4 oz	raisins
75 gm	.	3 oz	maraschino cherries, chopped
		1 tsp	cinnamon
		½ tsp	cloves

Peel oranges and lemons very thinly and cut peel into fine slivers. Discard white pith and chop the fruit, removing seeds. Combine peel and fruit pulp with remaining ingredients in a very large saucepan and bring to a boil. Cook until thick, stirring frequently. Pour into hot sterilized jars and seal.

COCOA FUDGE			
250 gm	.	10 oz	sugar
50 gm	.	2 oz	cocoa
		pinch	salt
165 ml	.	⅓ pt	milk
5 tsp	.	2 tbsp	butter
		½ tsp	vanilla essence
50 gm	.	2 oz	chopped nuts

Mix sugar, cocoa, salt and milk in saucepan and cook over direct heat, stirring occasionally, to soft-ball stage, or until cooking thermometer registers 234° F (112° C). Remove from heat, add butter and vanilla, and cool to lukewarm. Beat until mixture becomes stiff. Add nuts and pour onto buttered plate. Cut into squares.

CREAMY FUDGE *(Quick method)*			
165 ml	.	⅓ pt	evaporated milk
350 gm	.	14 oz	sugar
		½ tsp	salt
75 gm	.	3 oz	miniature marshmallows
300 gm	.	12 oz	semi-sweet chocolate pieces
		1 tsp	vanilla essence
50 gm	.	2 oz	chopped nuts

Mix milk, sugar and salt in saucepan and stir over medium heat until mixture boils. Continue cooking and stirring 5 minutes. Remove from heat and add marshmallows, chocolate and vanilla. Stir until smooth and completely blended. Add nuts and pour into buttered baking tin. Cool. Cut into squares.

DIVINITY

450 gm . 1 lb	sugar
140 ml . 1 gill	light corn syrup
6 tsp	water
2	egg whites
50 gm . 2 oz	chopped nuts
½ tsp	vanilla essence

Mix sugar, syrup and water in saucepan. Stir over medium heat until sugar dissolves. Cook without stirring to hard-ball stage, or until cooking thermometer registers 265°F (129°C). Beat egg whites until stiff. Continue beating while pouring hot syrup over them. Beat until mixture loses its shine and becomes very stiff. Add nuts and vanilla and pour into buttered baking tin. Cool. Cut into squares. Dust lightly with icing sugar and place between layers of waxed paper in covered container.

PENUCHE
COCONUT
BALLS
(Quick method)

125 ml . 1 gill	evaporated milk
400 gm . 1 lb	brown sugar
½ tsp	salt
100 gm . 4 oz	miniature marshmallows
2½ tsp . 1 tbsp	butter
300 gm . 12 oz	icing sugar, sieved
100 gm . 4 oz	desiccated coconut

Mix milk, sugar and salt in saucepan and stir over medium heat until mixture boils. Cook and stir 5 minutes. Remove from heat and add marshmallows and butter. Stir until smooth. Beat in icing sugar. Cool. Shape into 1-in. (25-mm) balls and roll in coconut.

ROCKY ROAD

200 gm . 8 oz	milk chocolate
100 gm . 4 oz	semi-sweet chocolate
25 gm . 1 oz	butter
50 gm . 2 oz	chopped nuts
50 gm . 2 oz	miniature marshmallows

Melt chocolate and butter together in top of double saucepan. Stir to blend. Spread nuts and marshmallows in buttered baking tin and pour chocolate mixture over them. Cool and cut into squares.

WASSAIL BOWL

1 l. .	1 qt	orange juice
1 l. .	1 qt	pineapple juice
250 ml .	½ pt	lemon juice
	1 piece	stick cinnamon
	7 . 8	whole cloves
100 gm .	4 oz	sugar
⅓ l. .	⅔ pt	Cognac brandy

Mix juices, spices and sugar in large saucepan. Bring to boil and simmer 30 minutes. Strain. Add brandy and pour into a punch bowl. Serve hot.
18-20 servings.

HOT BUTTERED RUM

3 tbsp	Hot Buttered Rum Batter
3 tbsp	rum
	boiling water
	nutmeg

Place batter and rum in a mug and fill with boiling water. Stir until well mixed. Sprinkle nutmeg on top.

Hot Buttered Rum Batter

100 gm .	4 oz	butter
3½ tbsp .	4 tbsp	icing sugar
5 tsp .	2 tbsp	rum
2½ tbsp .	3 tbsp	boiling water

Blend butter, icing sugar and rum with boiling water until very smooth. Cool.

TOM AND JERRY

3 tbsp	Tom and Jerry Batter
3 tbsp	brandy, rum or whisky
	hot milk
	nutmeg

Place batter and brandy in small mug or cup and mix well. Fill with hot milk and stir. Sprinkle nutmeg on top.

Tom and Jerry Batter

	4	eggs, separated
100 gm .	4 oz	sugar
	½ tsp	bicarbonate of soda

Beat egg yolks until thick. Beat egg whites, adding sugar and soda gradually, until stiff. Fold the two mixtures together.

EGG NOG

6 medium .	6 large	eggs, separated
75 gm .	3 oz	sugar
375 ml .	¾ pt	milk
125 ml .	1 gill	whisky
125 ml .	1 gill	rum
250 ml .	½ pt	thick cream, whipped
	1 tsp	nutmeg

Beat egg yolks until thick. Gradually beat in sugar. Add milk, whisky and rum and mix well. Beat egg whites until stiff and fold into the mixture. Add whipped cream and stir gently until blended. Pour into a punchbowl and sprinkle with nutmeg.

About 10 servings.

NON-ALCOHOLIC EGG NOG

Omit whisky and rum from above recipe and increase milk to 2½ pt (1½ l.)

CHRISTMAS CHEESE LOG

150 gm .	6 oz	Cheddar cheese, grated
100 gm .	4 oz	cream cheese
40 gm .	1½ oz	butter
	1 tsp	Worcestershire sauce
2½ tbsp ,	3 tbsp	milk
	½ tsp	salt
	¼ tsp	pepper
	dash	cayenne pepper
	4	pimento-stuffed green olives, sliced
		parsley sprigs
		paprika

Combine cheeses with butter until well blended. Add Worcestershire sauce, milk, salt, pepper and cayenne and mix well. Shape into a log and place on a small serving plate. Decorate with sliced stuffed olives and parsley sprigs and sprinkle lightly with paprika.

Serve as a spread for crackers.

Summertime Activities

Summer comes later to Minneapolis than to Seattle, and it never really leaves in Miami or Honolulu. But summer is an outdoor time everywhere. A time for swimming and sailing, for hiking and picnicking. Certain occasions stand out for Americans as traditional summertime celebrations for all.

INDEPENDENCE DAY CELEBRATIONS

John Adams, one of the Founding Fathers and Second President of the United States, said of the Fourth of July: 'I ... believe that it will be celebrated ... as the anniversary festival ... with shows, games, sports, guns, bells, bonfires and illuminations, from one end of the continent to the other ...'

Seventy-five years later, covered wagons were carrying the tradition of Independence Day celebrations across the prairies into the West. A report of one group of wagons, camped along the Oregon Trail, indicates that on 4 July the flag was raised and saluted with gunfire: the Declaration of Independence was read aloud; and the *Star Spangled Banner* was sung. The great feast which followed included roast antelope, antelope stew and antelope potpie; roast sage-hen, fried sage-hen and sage-hen stew; roast rabbit, fried rabbit and rabbit stew; potatoes, rolls, bread and Boston baked beans; pickles; dozens of cakes, including fruitcake and poundcake; a great variety of pies, including peach, strawberry, apple and custard; coffee, tea and chocolate; and a huge quantity of ice cream, made by using snow brought down from a nearby mountain.

Two hundred years after the signing of the Declaration of Independence, the celebrations and feasting continue. Many communities have special celebrations. In Biloxi, Mississippi, there is an annual Regatta; Alaska has a Mountain Marathon Race in Seward, and Eskimo Festivals in Nome and Kotzebue. Colorado has its Pikes Peak Auto Race, Oklahoma its Indian Stomp Dance, and New Mexico its Spanish Fiestas. In Albany, Oregon, loggers and lumberjacks compete at the Timber Carnival in tree climbing, log chopping, and log rolling on (and in) the pond. There are rodeos and round-ups, in Arcadia, Florida, in St Paul, Oregon, and in Silver City, New Mexico, not to mention those in small towns all across Wyoming and Texas, and a hundred places in between.

New Englanders celebrate with a traditional menu which includes clams, salmon, new potatoes, peas and Indian Pudding. For Western families there is often a backyard barbecue, or a picnic on the beach with wieners and marshmallows roasted over a bonfire. As the sun goes down, the rockets and Roman candles burst into the sky in a gigantic display of fireworks from Boston to San Francisco.

BARBECUED
BEEF KEBABS

140 ml .	1 gill	dry red wine
	2 tbsp	salad oil
	2 tbsp	lemon juice
	1 clove	garlic, crushed
	¼ tsp	salt
	⅛ tsp	pepper
	¼ tsp	basil
900 gm .	2 lb	frying steak, cubed
	12 small	onions
	12 small	mushrooms
	1	green pepper

Mix wine, oil, lemon juice, garlic, salt, pepper and basil and pour over the steak cubes. Refrigerate 24 hours, turning meat occasionally. Peel onions and boil them 10 minutes; drain and cool. Remove seeds of the green pepper and cut it into squares. On each of six long skewers place meat cubes, alternated with onions, mushrooms and green pepper squares. Brush with marinade and grill over hot barbecue coals until well done on all sides.
  Serves 6.

STEAK
BARBECUE

900 gm, 12 mm thick		
2 lb, ½ in. thick		stewing steak
275 ml .	½ pt	vinegar
275 ml .	½ pt	water
	2 tbsp	salad oil
	1 tbsp	lemon juice
	1 tsp	salt
	1 tbsp	sugar
	½ tsp	basil
	½ tsp	oregano
	¼ tsp	pepper
	1	onion, minced

Cut steak into serving size pieces. Place in a shallow dish. Combine remaining ingredients and pour over the meat. Cover and refrigerate 24 hours, turning meat occasionally. Remove meat from marinade and grill over hot barbecue coals, basting frequently with marinade.
  Serves 4.

| **BARBECUED** | *2 kg* . 4-5 lb | pork spareribs |
| **SPARERIBS** | | Red Barbecue Sauce |

Brush ribs on both sides with sauce. Grill slowly over moderately hot coals, basting frequently until well done on both sides. (1-1½ hours).
Serves 4.

RED BARBECUE	*275 ml* . ½ pt	ketchup
SAUCE	6 tbsp	vinegar
	3 tbsp	salad oil
	25 gm . 1 oz	brown sugar
	140 ml . 1 gill	water
	¼ tsp	mustard powder
	¼ tsp	salt
	2 tbsp	Worcestershire sauce
	1 small	onion, minced

Combine all ingredients in small saucepan and simmer for 15 minutes, stirring frequently. Use for basting pork, chicken, etc. in barbecue recipes.

| **BARBECUED** | 2 small | frying chickens, split into halves |
| **CHICKEN** | | Red Barbecue Sauce |

Brush chicken halves on both sides with sauce and place, skin side up, on barbecue grill. Grill over moderately hot coals, for 30 minutes, basting frequently with sauce. Turn chicken and cook other side in same way.
Serves 4.

BARBECUED	*450 gm* . 1 lb	minced raw beef
HAMBURGERS	2 tbsp	minced onion
	¾ tsp	salt
	⅛ tsp	pepper
	180 ml . ⅓ pt	tomato ketchup
	1 tsp	Worcestershire sauce
	4	hamburger buns, split

Combine beef, onion, salt and pepper and press into four flat patties. Mix ketchup and Worcestershire sauce in a small saucepan and warm it on the edge of the barbecue. Warm the buns, or toast them on the cut side only. Grill patties over hot barbecue coals until done on both sides. Spoon sauce over meat and serve in warm buns.

HAMBURGER PACKETS

450 gm . 1 lb	raw minced beef
1	onion, sliced
2	potatoes, sliced
1	green pepper, sliced
4 tbsp	bacon drippings or butter
	salt and pepper

Divide beef into four patties and place each on a large square of aluminium foil. Sprinkle with salt and pepper and arrange onions, potatoes and green pepper strips on top of meat. Sprinkle lightly with salt and pepper and top with a pat of bacon fat or butter. Bring corners of foil up over and fold together. Place foil packets directly on hot barbecue coals and cook 1 hour.
  Serves 4.

POTATOES IN FOIL

675 gm . 1½ lb	potatoes, peeled and diced
1 small	onion, chopped
1 tbsp	chopped parsley
	salt and pepper
4 tbsp	butter

Place potatoes on a large piece of heavy foil. Scatter the chopped onion and parsley over, sprinkle with salt and pepper and dot with butter. Bring foil up over and seal with double fold. Fold ends of foil over twice and turn upward. Place the sealed packet on the back of the barbecue grill and cook 1 hour.

CORN IN FOIL

whole ears of fresh sweet corn
butter
salt and pepper

Remove husks and silk from corn and place each ear on a square of foil. Spread generously with butter, sprinkle with salt and pepper, and roll up in the foil. Place foil packets *directly on hot coals*. Turn with tongs after 10 minutes and cook 10 minutes longer.

POTATO SALAD

675 gm . 1½ lb	potatoes
5	eggs, hard-boiled
1 stick	celery
2	spring onions
1½ tsp	salt
140 ml . 1 gill	mayonnaise
1½ tbsp	vinegar
1 tbsp	sugar
2 tbsp	milk
¼ tsp	mustard powder
	paprika

Boil potatoes in their skins until tender. Cool. Remove skins and dice potatoes. Dice four of the eggs and chop the celery and onions. Mix salt, mayonnaise, vinegar, sugar, milk and mustard powder. Combine mayonnaise mixture with the potatoes, eggs, celery and onions, and mix gently. Spoon into a salad bowl. Slice remaining egg and arrange on top. Sprinkle paprika over all. Cover and chill.

Serves 8.

MACARONI SALAD

Follow directions for Potato Salad but use 5 oz (140 gm) short macaroni pieces in place of potatoes. Cook until barely tender; drain. Combine with remaining ingredients and chill.

BEAN SALAD

450 gm . 1 lb	tinned green beans, drained
450 gm . 1 lb	tinned chickpeas, drained
450 gm . 1 lb	tinned red kidney beans, drained
1	green pepper, chopped
1	onion, chopped
50 gm . 2 oz	sugar
140 ml . 1 gill	vinegar
5 tbsp	salad oil
1 tsp	salt
¼ tsp	pepper

Combine drained vegetables with green pepper and onion. Mix remaining ingredients and pour over. Mix thoroughly and chill overnight. Toss before serving.

Serves 12.

FRESH FRUIT SALAD

½	melon, cubed
2	peaches, peeled and sliced
150 gm . 6 oz	fresh raspberries
150 gm . 6 oz	seedless grapes

Arrange fruits on a large plate or in a large shallow dish Drizzle Honey-Lime Salad Dressing over the salad.

Serves 4.

HONEY-LIME	5 tbsp	honey
SALAD	5 tbsp	lime juice
DRESSING	5 tbsp	salad oil

Place in a jar and shake well until blended. Chill. Use as a salad dressing on any fruit salad.

ICED TEA

strong tea
ice cubes
lemon juice
sugar

Prepare tea and strain into jug. Allow to cool. Fill tall glasses with ice cubes and pour the tea over them. Add lemon juice and sugar to taste and stir.

ICED COFFEE

strong coffee
ice cubes
sugar

Pour coffee into a jug and allow to cool. Fill glasses with ice cubes and pour coffee over them. Add sugar to taste.

THE 1890s ICE CREAM PARLOUR

Any time is ice cream time in the United States, but summertime especially.

A highlight of the Victorian Era in America was the ice cream parlour. In the twentieth century this gave way to the drug store soda fountain. Few drug stores have fountains today, but the Victorian ice cream parlour has made a comeback, complete with red velvet draperies, player pianos which churn out jazzy melodies, and waiters in straw boaters. Parlours compete with each other to produce the biggest and most outlandish concoctions, with names like The Zoo, The Trough, The Whole Thing. The old standbys are there also. There are sodas and milk shakes, chocolate, strawberry, vanilla or a dozen other flavours. There are ice cream sundaes topped with strawberry, caramel or pineapple, or rich hot fudge; and an old-fashioned banana split still has three flavours of ice cream, three kinds of topping, whipped cream and nuts, and as many calories as ever.

BANANA SPLIT

1 scoop	vanilla ice cream
1 scoop	strawberry ice cream
1 scoop	chocolate ice cream
1	banana, halved lengthwise
1 tbsp	apricot or pineapple jam
1 tbsp	strawberry or raspberry jam
3 tbsp	sweetened whipped cream
1 tsp	chopped nuts
1	maraschino cherry

Place the three scoops of ice cream in a row on a plate, chocolate in the centre. Place banana halves along sides. Spoon apricot jam over strawberry ice cream and strawberry jam over vanilla. Spoon whipped cream over top, sprinkle with nuts and top with the cherry.

CHOCOLATE SUNDAE

1 large scoop	vanilla ice cream
3 tbsp	Chocolate Sauce
1 tsp	chopped nuts

Place ice cream in a parfait glass or dessert dish and spoon sauce over it. Sprinkle with nuts.

CHOCOLATE SAUCE

150 gm .	6 oz	semi-sweet chocolate pieces
125 ml .	1 gill	light corn syrup
3½ tbsp .	4 tbsp	evaporated milk
2½ tsp .	1 tbsp	butter
	½ tsp	vanilla essence

Place all ingredients in top of double saucepan over hot water and stir until completely blended. Serve over ice cream or cake.
  4 servings.

STRAWBERRY SUNDAE

1 large scoop	vanilla ice cream
6 large	strawberries
2 tsp	sugar
1 tbsp	sweetened whipped cream
2 tsp	chopped nuts
1	maraschino cherry

Place ice cream in a parfait glass or dessert dish. Crush the berries with the sugar and spoon over ice cream. Place whipped cream on top, sprinkle with nuts and top with cherry.

HOT FUDGE	1 large scoop	vanilla ice cream
SUNDAE	4 tbsp	Hot Fudge Sauce
	1 tsp	chopped nuts

Place 1 tablespoon of Hot Fudge Sauce in a parfait glass or dessert dish. Add a scoop of ice cream and spoon remaining sauce over the top. Sprinkle with nuts.

HOT FUDGE	200 gm . 8 oz	semi-sweet chocolate
SAUCE	250 ml . ½ pt	milk
	75 gm . 3 oz	sugar

Place chocolate and milk in saucepan over medium heat and cook until thick. Add sugar slowly and cook until smooth, stirring frequently. Serve hot over ice cream or cake.

HOT FUDGE	4 large	Brownies (see p. 183)
BROWNIE	4 scoops	vanilla ice cream
SUNDAE	4 tbsp	Hot Fudge Sauce or
		Chocolate Sauce

Place warm Brownies on four small dessert plates. Top with ice cream and pour Hot Fudge Sauce over the top.
    Serves 4.

TUTTI-FRUTTI	1 l. . 1 qt	vanilla ice cream
	2½ tbsp . 3 tbsp	brandy or sherry
	100 gm . 4 oz	chopped candied peel
	50 gm . 2 oz	chopped candied cherries

Allow ice cream to soften slightly. Mix brandy with peel and cherries and stir into ice cream until well blended. Return to freezer.

| CHOCOLATE | 180 ml . ⅓ pt | milk |
| MILK SHAKE | 1 scoop | chocolate ice cream |

Place in liquidizer and blend until smooth. Pour into a tall glass and serve with a straw.

Substitute strawberry ice cream in above recipe.

ICE CREAM SODA	4 tbsp	crushed fruit or fruit-flavoured syrup
		plain soda water
	1 scoop	ice cream

Place fruit or syrup in tall glass and half-fill glass with soda water. Stir to blend. Add ice cream and fill glass to top with soda water. Serve with a straw and a long spoon.

| **FLOAT** | chilled carbonated beverage, such as cola or fizzy lemonade |
| | vanilla ice cream |

Pour beverage into tall glass, leaving space at top for ice cream. Slide a scoop of ice cream carefully onto top of beverage. Serve with straw and long spoon.

THE STATE FAIR: CATTLE EXHIBITS, CARNIVAL RIDES, AND CAKE CONTESTS

Across the country, as the warm summer days shorten into autumn, the State Fairs begin. Into the giant barns and sheds come the cattle and sheep, the horses, poultry and rabbits, to compete for the blue ribbons. Cakes, pies, jams and pickles are brought for judging in the food halls; and handicrafts, paintings and photography are exhibited in other halls. In the industrial exhibit tents are the latest inventions, with here and there a glimpse of the future.

People wander through the outdoor exhibits of flowers and shrubs and swimming pools. They pause inside a barn to look tenderly at a tiny lamb, only hours old, or to admire in awe a giant Black Angus bull. In the stadium, spectators watch horseracing or a rodeo, and on the outdoor stage musicians and actors perform to a packed lawn.

Sooner or later, everyone winds up on the Midway. The calliopes grind out their raucous melodies as children ride proud merry-go-round horses or sweep skyward on the ferris wheel. The crack of rifles in the shooting gallery mingles with the shouts of hawkers and vendors and the roar of the roller coaster. The warm air is scented — a peculiar spicy blend of hot dogs and hamburgers, cotton candy and chocolate; coffee and cola and lemonade.

CONEY ISLAND
HOT DOGS

225 gm .	8 oz	minced raw beef
	1 small	onion, chopped
	1 tbsp	flour
140 ml .	1 gill	tomato purée
	½ tsp	chilli powder
	½ tsp	salt
	4	frankfurter sausages
	4	hot dog rolls, heated

Stir the beef and onion over medium heat until lightly browned. Stir in flour. Add tomato purée, chilli powder and salt. Simmer 10 minutes. Place sausages in pan and cover with cold water. Bring to boil and simmer 5 minutes; drain. Split rolls not quite through and place a frankfurter and a quarter of the sauce in each.
Serves 4.

HAMBURGERS
DE LUXE

450 gm .	1 lb	lean minced raw beef
		salt and pepper
	1	onion, thinly sliced (optional)
	1 large	tomato, thinly sliced
	4	lettuce leaves
	2 tbsp	chopped sweet pickled gherkins
	2 tbsp	mayonnaise
	4	hamburger buns, warmed and buttered

Shape meat into four balls and flatten between sheets of plastic or foil. Patties should be slightly larger in diameter than buns as they will shrink when cooked. Sprinkly lightly with salt and pepper and fry or grill on both sides. On bottom half of each bun place meat patty, slices of raw onion, sliced tomato and lettuce. Mix chopped pickle and mayonnaise and spread on top halves of buns. Serve immediately.
Serves 4.

CHEESEBURGERS

Follow directions for Hamburgers above, but cook meat patties on one side, turn them and place a thin slice of cheese over each patty. Complete cooking and assemble as for Hamburgers.

SLOPPY JOE	*450 g* . 1 lb	minced raw beef
HAMBURGERS	1 small	onion, chopped
	½	green pepper, chopped
	180 ml . ⅓ pt	tomato purée
	1 tsp	salt
	1½ tsp	chilli powder
	4	hamburger buns, split and toasted

Stir beef, onion and green pepper over medium heat until browned. Add purée, salt and chilli powder and simmer 10 minutes. Spoon onto toasted buns.

Serves 4.

CORN DOGS	*65 gm* . 2½ oz	plain flour
	65 gm . 2½ oz	yellow cornmeal
	1 tsp . 1¼ tsp	baking powder
	½ tsp	salt
	125 ml . 1 gill	milk
	1	egg, beaten
	4 tsp . 1½ tbsp	cooking oil
	300 gm . 12 oz	frankfurter sausages
		wooden skewers
		oil for deep frying

Mix flour, cornmeal, baking powder, salt. Combine milk, egg and oil and blend with dry ingredients. Heat oil to 375°F (190°C). Run a 6-in. (15-cm) skewer lengthwise into each frankfurter. Dip in batter and fry until golden-brown and crisp.

Serves 4.

PRONTO PUPS

Omit yellow cornmeal from Corn Dog recipe but increase flour to 5 oz (130 gm).

POPSICLES

Orange juice or any other fruit
juice or fruit-flavoured drink
small wooden skewers
small paper cups

Pour juice into cups and stand a skewer in each one. Freeze until hard.
Remove paper.

SNOW CONES

finely crushed ice
concentrated fruit syrup
Small paper cups or cones

Pile ice into paper cups and drizzle 1 or 2 tablespoons of syrup over top.

Parties Around the American Calendar

For most Americans, each year begins and ends with a celebration, and every month brings at least one special day.

New Year's Day may be a small family dinner or an Open House for a hundred, but baked ham is traditionally served.

Lincoln's Birthday on 12 February is celebrated with a cake or ice cream in the shape of a log, commemorating his birth in a simple log cabin.

Valentine's Day means sending cards, Sweetheart Balls, and heart-shaped candy, cookies and cakes.

George Washington's Birthday is on 22 February. He is said to have confessed to cutting down a cherry tree, and millions of cherry pies are baked on this date.

St Patrick's Day on 17 March is the day when almost everyone remembers an Irish great-grandmother and wears a shamrock or a green hat or sweater. There are lots of parties, New York City has a big parade, and people everywhere eat corned beef and cabbage or Irish Stew.

Shrove Tuesday is the culmination of *Mardi Gras* festivities in the South, especially in New Orleans where the pre-Lent feasting goes on for two weeks.

Hot Cross Buns are served not only on *Good Friday* but throughout the Lenten season.

Easter is a joyous celebration for Christians, and also a day for big family gatherings. Small children wake to find baskets of chocolate eggs brought by the Easter Bunny. Later they hunt for coloured eggs hidden throughout the house. Dinner usually includes roast leg of lamb or baked ham, and a cake baked in the shape of a lamb, a rabbit or a giant egg.

Memorial Day on 30 May, also called Decoration Day, is the time for carrying flowers to the graves, followed by family reunions and picnics.

June is the traditional month for *Weddings*. Brides-to-be are honoured at parties or 'showers' where they are given kitchen utensils or lingerie. The wedding rehearsal is followed by a special dinner, and the wedding day festivities include champagne or punch and a three-tiered cake.

June is also the month for *Graduation* parties as students receive high school diplomas and college degrees.

Summer progresses through *Independence Day* and *Labor Day* with picnics and barbecues.

No special date is needed for a *Card Party*, whether it be a foursome for luncheon and bridge, or a fund-raising event for hundreds, and every day is someone's *Birthday*.

Autumn brings cooler days and parties move indoors for *Potluck Suppers* where everyone brings a casserole or salad, or a pie or cake.

October ends with *Halloween*. Giant pumpkins, hollowed and carved and with lighted candles inside, become Jack o'Lanterns glowing on front porches. Small children dressed as goblins and witches go from door to door crying: 'Trick or treat?' and carrying bags to be filled with sweets. Older children attend costume parties where they are served doughnuts and caramel apples and apple juice.

Autumn is *Football* season and pizza is popular at after-game parties.

November brings *Thanksgiving* with turkey and cranberries and pumpkin pie.

December brings *Hanukkah* and the *Christmas* season with its succession of cocktail parties and dinners.

The year ends with *New Year's Eve* parties where dancing and revelry culminate in a midnight breakfast and the start of another year.

NEW YEAR'S   *4-6 kg* . 10-14 lb   ham (whole)
HAM WITH
RAISIN SAUCE

Place ham, fat side up, on a rack in roasting tin. Bake in a very moderate oven (325°F, 170°C, Gas Mark 3) allowing 20 minutes per pound (22 minutes per half-kilo). Remove from oven and allow to stand 20 minutes before carving. Serve with Raisin Sauce.

RAISIN SAUCE   *100 gm* . 4 oz   brown sugar
2½ tsp . 1 tbsp   cornflour
190 ml . 1½ gills   water
2½ tsp . 1 tbsp   lemon juice
50 gm . 2 oz   raisins

Combine brown sugar and cornflour and gradually add water. Add lemon juice and raisins and cook over medium heat, stirring, until thickened. Serve with ham.

WASHINGTON'S			shortcrust pastry for
BIRTHDAY			two-crust pie
CHERRY PIE	*675 gm* .	1½ lb	fresh sour cherries
	115 gm .	4 oz	sugar
		4 tbsp	plain flour
		¼ tsp	almond essence
		1 tbsp	butter

Prepare pastry, using half to line a 9-in. (23-cm) pie plate. Stone cherries and combine them with the sugar, flour and almond essence. Mix well. Pour into pastry and dot with butter. Cover with top crust, seal and crimp edges and cut several small slits in the top. Bake in a hot oven (450°F, 230°C, Gas Mark 8) for 10 minutes. Reduce heat (350°F, 180°C, Gas Mark 4) and bake 30 minutes.

IRISH CORNED	*2 kg* .	4-5 lb	silverside of beef
BEEF DINNER		1	onion, quartered
		1 tbsp	peppercorns
		1	head cabbage, shredded

Cook beef with onion and peppercorns in water to cover until tender (about 3 hours). Remove beef to platter and keep warm. Place cabbage in large saucepan and cover with some of the liquid (strained) in which beef was cooked. Bring to boil and simmer, covered, 5 minutes. Drain and arrange cabbage around meat.

EASTER EGGS	2 dozen	hard-boiled eggs
	1 tsp each	red, blue, green and
		yellow food-colouring
		warm water

Place red food-colouring and 1/3 pt (165 ml) warm water in a small deep basin. Immerse six eggs, two or three at a time, in the red solution until desired shade of pink has been reached. Repeat with remaining eggs and colours, dyeing six eggs in each colour.

ROAST LEG OF	*2½ kg* .	5-6 lb	leg of lamb
LAMB		1 tsp	salt
		1 tsp	crumbled rosemary
		¼ tsp	pepper
		⅛ tsp	garlic powder

Mix salt, rosemary, pepper and garlic powder and rub mixture over the surface of the lamb. Place lamb, fat side up, on a rack in a roasting tin. Bake, uncovered, in a very moderate oven (325° F, 170° C, Gas Mark 3) for 3-3½ hours.

WEDDING OR	*300 gm* . 12 oz	plain flour
BIRTHDAY	*4 tsp* . 4½ tsp	baking powder
CAKE	¼ tsp	salt
	75 gm . 3 oz	butter or margarine
	250 gm . 10 oz	sugar
	2	eggs
	250 ml . ½ pt	milk
	1¼ tsp . 1½ tsp	vanilla essence

Sieve flour, baking powder and salt together. Cream butter with sugar and beat in eggs, one at a time. Add dry ingredients alternately with milk. Add vanilla. Grease and dust with flour three 9-in. (23-cm) sandwich tins and divide batter between them. Bake in a moderate oven (375° F, 190° C, Gas Mark 5) until done (about 25 minutes). Cool. Stack layers with Lemon Filling between. Ice top and sides with Butter Cream Frosting.

LEMON FILLING	6 tbsp	cornflour
	½ tsp	salt
	225 gm . 8 oz	sugar
	6	egg yolks
	550 ml . 1 pt	water
	6 tbsp	lemon juice

Mix cornflour, salt, sugar with egg yolks. Gradually add water and lemon juice. Cook, stirring, over medium heat until thickened. Cool. Use as filling between layers of Wedding or Birthday cake or any three-layer cake.

For two-layer cake halve quantities of above recipe.

BUTTER CREAM	*150 gm* . 6 oz	butter, softened
FROSTING	*2½ tbsp* . 3 tbsp	milk
	1¾ tsp . 2 tsp	vanilla essence
	450 gm . 18 oz	icing sugar

Blend butter, milk and vanilla and beat in sugar gradually. Beat until smooth. Use as frosting for three-layer cake.

Tinted Frosting

Add a few drops of food-colouring to above recipe.

Orange Butter Cream Frosting

Substitute orange juice for milk and omit vanilla in above recipe.

Lemon Butter Cream Frosting

Substitute lemon juice for milk and omit vanilla.

CHAMPAGNE
PUNCH

2 bottles	champagne, chilled
1 l. 1 qt	ginger ale chilled
	ice cubes

Combine in a punchbowl and serve in champagne glasses.

PINK PARTY
PUNCH

2 l. 2 qt	carbonated lemonade
1 l. 1 qt	apple juice
1 l. 1 qt	strawberry ice cream
	ice cubes

Combine in a punchbowl and stir until the ice cream is partially melted. Serve in small punch cups.
   Approximately 20 servings.

RIBBON
SANDWICH LOAF

1 large loaf	unsliced white bread
	Egg Salad Filling
	Chicken Salad Filling
	Tuna Salad Filling
200 gm. 8 oz	softened cream cheese
	sliced olives and
	parsley for garnish

Remove crusts from loaf and cut into four horizontal layers. Spread each of three layers with a different filling, leaving top layer plain. Re-assemble loaf. Ice top and sides of loaf with cream cheese and decorate with sliced olives and parsley. Chill thoroughly. To serve: slice as for an ordinary loaf.

CHICKEN SALAD	55 gm . 2 oz	chopped cooked chicken
SANDWICH	½ stick	celery, finely chopped
FILLING	½ tsp	lemon juice
	⅛ tsp	salt
	⅛ tsp	pepper
	1½ tbsp	mayonnaise

Combine chicken, celery, lemon juice, salt, pepper and mayonnaise and mix well. Use as filling for two sandwiches, or for one layer of filling of Ribbon Sandwich Loaf.

EGG SALAD	2	hard-boiled eggs
SANDWICH	1½ tbsp	chopped celery
FILLING	1 tbsp	chopped green pepper
	¼ tsp	salt
	dash	pepper
	1½ tbsp	mayonnaise
	2 tsp	sweet pickle relish

Mash eggs with a fork and combine with remaining ingredients. Mix well. Use as filling for two sandwiches, or as filling for one layer of Ribbon Sandwich Loaf.

TUNA SALAD	75 gm . 3 oz	tinned tuna, drained
SANDWICH	1 tbsp	finely chopped celery
FILLING	2 tsp	finely chopped spring onion
	1 tsp	pickle relish
	1 tbsp	mayonnaise
	dash	pepper

Combine all ingredients and mix well with a fork. Use as filling for two sandwiches or as filling for one layer of Ribbon Sandwich Loaf.

DE LUXE	565 gm . 20 oz	tinned fruit cocktail, drained
FRUIT	2	bananas, sliced
SALAD	100 gm . 4 oz	miniature marshmallows
	275 ml . ½ pt	cream, whipped

Combine fruits and marshmallows. Gently stir in whipped cream until well blended. Chill 1 hour.
Serves 8.

DEVILLED EGGS

4	eggs, hard-boiled
¼ tsp	mustard powder
1 tsp	vinegar
⅛ tsp	pepper
¼ tsp	salt
1 tbsp	mayonnaise
	paprika
	parsley

Cut eggs in halves lengthwise. Remove yolks and mash them with other ingredients. Pile mixture back into whites and arrange on a serving plate. Sprinkle lightly with paprika and garnish with parsley.

DOUGHNUTS

175 gm .	7 oz	plain flour
1¾ tsp .	2 tsp	baking powder
	¼ tsp	nutmeg
	½ tsp	salt
	1	egg
100 ml .	1 gill (scant)	milk
85 gm .	3½ oz	sugar
2½ tsp .	1 tbsp	melted butter
		sugar or icing sugar

Sieve flour, baking powder, nutmeg and salt together. Beat egg with milk and sugar. Stir in melted butter and dry ingredients. Turn out onto a floured board and knead lightly, working in a little more flour if dough is too sticky to handle. Roll out to ½-in. (12-mm) thickness and cut into 3-in. (8-cm) circles. Cut a 1-in. (25-mm) circle from the centre of each. Fry the Doughnuts in deep hot fat (360°F, 185°C) until brown on bottom. Turn carefully and brown other side. Remove from fat carefully and drain on paper towels. Roll in sugar or icing sugar. The small centres can be re-rolled and cut as Doughnuts, or fried as Doughnut Holes.

CARAMEL APPLES

	4	apples, medium size
	4	wooden sticks
340 gm .	12 oz	soft caramels
	2 tbsp	water

Wash and dry apples. Place caramels and water in top of double saucepan and cook over hot water until melted, stirring frequently. Push a stick into each apple and twirl in hot caramel until well coated. Stand apples on buttered plate until cool.

HOT SPICED	1½ l. . 3 pt	apple juice
APPLE JUICE	1 piece	stick cinnamon
	11 . 12	whole cloves
	11 . 12	whole allspice berries
	50 gm . 2 oz	brown sugar
	¼ tsp	nutmeg

Combine all ingredients in a large saucepan and bring to a boil slowly. Simmer 15 minutes. Strain. Serve hot.
    8 servings.

PIZZA	150 gm . 6 oz	raw minced beef
	100 gm . 4 oz	plain flour
	½ tsp	salt
	1 tsp	baking powder
	65 ml . ½ gill	milk
	5 tsp : 2 tbsp	cooking oil
	3½ tbsp . 4 tbsp	grated Parmesan cheese
	165 ml . ⅓ pt	tomato purée
	⅛ tsp	oregano
	⅛ tsp	thyme
	¼ tsp	pepper
	4	mushrooms, sliced
	6	black olives, stoned and sliced
	3 tbsp	chopped raw onion
	100 gm . 4 oz	Mozzarella cheese, cut into thin strips

Stir minced beef in a frying pan until lightly browned. Drain off excess fat. Mix flour, salt and baking powder. Combine milk with oil and stir into flour mixture. Roll dough on a floured board to a large circle, at least 12 in. (30 cm) in diameter. Place on a baking sheet and crimp edges to form a raised border. Mix Parmesan cheese, tomato purée, oregano, thyme and pepper and spread over surface. Distribute cooked beef, mushrooms, olives and onion evenly over surface. Lay Mozzarella cheese strips on top and bake in a moderately hot oven (425°F, 220°C, Gas Mark 7) for 20 minutes. Cut into wedges.
    Serves 3 or 4.

COCKTAILS

TOM COLLINS

3 tbsp	gin
1½ tsp	castor sugar
1½ tbsp	lemon juice
	soda water
	ice cubes

Combine gin, sugar and lemon juice in a cocktail shaker and shake well. Fill a tall glass with ice cubes and pour the mixture over. Fill with soda water and stir.

Vodka Collins

Use vodka in place of gin in above recipe.

BLOODY MARY

3 tbsp	vodka
½ tsp	lemon juice
¼ tsp	Worcestershire sauce
1-3 drops	hot pepper sauce, or dash pepper
	ice cubes
	tomato juice

Combine vodka, lemon juice, Worcestershire and pepper sauce in a shaker and shake well. Pour over four ice cubes in a glass and fill with tomato juice. Stir.

MARTINI

3 tbsp	gin
2 tsp	dry vermouth
	crushed ice
1 or 2	green olives

Combine gin, vermouth and ice and stir. Strain into a cocktail glass and add olives.

SCREWDRIVER

3 tbsp	vodka
	orange juice
4 or 5	ice cubes

Place ice cubes in a medium-sized glass tumbler and add vodka. Fill with orange juice and stir.

WHISKY SOUR

3 tbsp	whisky
1 tbsp	lemon juice
1 tsp	icing sugar
3 or 4	ice cubes

Combine in a cocktail shaker, shake well and strain into a cocktail glass.

MANHATTAN

3 tbsp	whisky (preferably bourbon whiskey)
1 tbsp	sweet vermouth
dash	Angostura bitters
	crushed ice
	maraschino cherry

Combine whisky, vermouth, bitters and ice and stir. Strain into a cocktail glass and add a cherry.

DAIQUIRI

3 tbsp	rum
1 tbsp	lime juice
1 tsp	icing sugar
	crushed ice

Combine in a cocktail shaker, shake well and strain into a cocktail glass.

HIGHBALL

3 tbsp	whisky
	ginger ale or other carbonated beverage
4 or 5	ice cubes

Place ice cubes in tall glass, add whisky and fill with beverage. Stir.

HARVEY WALLBANGER

3 tbsp	vodka
1 tbsp	Galliano liqueur
	orange juice
	ice cubes

129

Pour vodka and Galliano into a tall glass. Fill with ice cubes and pour orange juice over. Do not stir.

BRANDY   2 tbsp   brandy
ALEXANDER   2 tbsp   crème de cacao
                    2 tbsp   cream
                             ice

Shake well and strain into a cocktail glass.

PINK LADY   3 tbsp   gin
                    1½ tbsp   lemon juice
                     1 tbsp   grenadine
                          1   egg white
                              crushed ice

Shake well and strain into a cocktail glass.

GRASSHOPPER   3 tbsp   white crème de cacao
                     3 tbsp   green crème de menthe
                     1 tbsp   thick cream
                          4   ice cubes

Shake in a cocktail shaker and strain into a glass.

STINGER   3 tbsp   brandy
                     3 tbsp   white crème de menthe
                              ice

Shake well and strain into a glass.

PARTY SNACKS

MARINATED
MUSHROOMS

2 dozen	small whole mushrooms
4 tbsp	salad oil
4 tbsp	water
4 tbsp	vinegar
1 tbsp	lemon juice
2 tsp	sugar
1 tbsp	minced onion
½ tsp	salt
⅛ tsp	cayenne pepper
⅛ tsp	garlic powder
pinch	thyme
pinch	tarragon
1 tbsp	chopped parsley

Wash mushrooms and cut off stems. Combine all remaining ingredients except parsley in a saucepan. Add mushrooms and bring to a boil. Simmer 10 minutes. Cool. Add parsley and refrigerate, covered, for one or two days before serving.

CLAM DIP

| 175 gm . 6 oz | tinned minced clams, undrained |
| 225 gm . 8 oz | cream cheese, softened |

Combine and mix thoroughly. Serve with potato crisps or raw vegetables.

PARTY NIBBLES

25 gm . 1 oz	melted butter
50 gm . 2 oz	bite-size shredded wheat
50 gm . 2 oz	puffed rice
100 gm . 4 oz	mixed nuts
100 gm . 4 oz	salted peanuts
¼ tsp	garlic powder
½ tsp	Worcestershire sauce

Toss all ingredients together and place in large baking tin. Bake in a moderate oven (350°F, 180°C, Gas Mark 4) for 15 minutes. Cool and store in a covered tin.

KABOBS

Cheddar cheese cubes
pickle chunks
black olives, stoned
salami or ham cubes
pickled onions
stuffed green olives

Choose at least four items from list above. Using wooden toothpicks as skewers, place one of each of them on each pick. Arrange Kabobs on a plate, sunburst fashion, cover and chill until serving time.

CALORIE COUNTER'S DIP

550 ml .	1 pt	cottage cheese
	2 tbsp	dry onion soup mix

Press cottage cheese through a sieve. Add soup mix and stir until blended. Chill 1-2 hours. Serve with raw vegetables (carrots, celery, cauliflower, mushrooms, turnips, cucumbers, courgettes).

BACON-WRAPPED CHICKEN LIVERS

12	chicken livers
12 thin rashers	streaky bacon, halved

Separate lobes of livers and remove any fat. Wrap each piece in a half slice of bacon and secure with a wooden toothpick. Place on a rack in a pan and grill until bacon is crisp and brown. Turn and grill other side. Serve hot.
    24 snacks.

STUFFED MUSHROOMS

	12 large	mushrooms
	2 tbsp	butter, melted
50 gm .	2 oz	Cheddar cheese, grated
	3 tbsp	fine dry breadcrumbs
	2 tbsp	butter
	¼ tsp	pepper

Remove stems from mushrooms. Wash and dry caps and place rounded side up in a baking tin. Brush tops with melted butter and grill until lightly browned. Mix cheese, crumbs, butter and pepper. Turn mushrooms and fill with cheese mixture. Return to grill and grill until browned. Serve hot.

MIDNIGHT	100 gm . 4 oz	plain flour
BREAKFAST	2¼ tsp . 2½ tsp	baking powder
PANCAKES	¼ tsp	salt
	3½ tsp . 4 tsp	sugar
	1	egg, beaten
	165 ml . ⅓ pt	milk
	4 tbsp . 5 tbsp	oil

Sieve flour with baking powder, salt and sugar. Combine egg with milk and oil and stir in flour mixture. Beat until smooth. Pour onto hot, lightly greased griddle or frying pan, using four tablespoons for each pancake. Cook until bottom is browned and top looks slightly dry. Turn and brown other side. Serve with butter and maple syrup, pancake syrup, honey or golden syrup.

8 pancakes.

PANCAKE AND	200 gm . 8 oz	brown sugar
WAFFLE SYRUP	250 ml . ½ pt	water
	¼ tsp	salt

Mix in saucepan and simmer gently 10 minutes. Cool.

PART II

General Recipes

Soups and Chowders

CREAM OF CHICKEN SOUP

	3 tbsp	chicken fat or butter
	4 tbsp	plain flour
550 ml .	1 pt	chicken broth
275 ml .	½ pt	cream or milk
	1½ tsp	salt
	¼ tsp	pepper
50 gm .	2 oz	boneless cooked chicken, diced very fine

Melt fat and stir in flour. Gradually add broth and cream. Add remaining ingredients and stir over low heat until thickened and smooth.
Serves 4.

Cream of Turkey Soup

Substitute cooked turkey for chicken in above recipe.

POTATO SOUP WITH HAM

100 gm .	4 oz	cooked ham
	1	onion, diced
675 gm .	1½ lb	potatoes, peeled and diced
550 ml .	1 pt	water
	2 tsp	salt
	¼ tsp	pepper
360 ml .	⅔ pt	milk
	1 tbsp	finely chopped parsley

Cut fat from ham and dice it. Cut lean part of ham into small cubes. Fry onion and ham fat together until tender. (If ham is lean, substitute 1 tablespoon butter.) Add potatoes, water and salt and simmer, covered, 30 minutes. Add pepper, milk and ham and heat but do not boil. Add parsley.
6 servings.

CHEESE SOUP

	4 tbsp	butter
	1	onion, finely chopped
	4 tbsp	plain flour
550 ml .	1 pt	milk
400 ml .	¾ pt	water
	1½ tsp	salt
	⅛ tsp	pepper
75 gm .	3 oz	Cheddar cheese, cubed
	2 tbsp	chopped parsley

Fry onion in butter until tender. Stir in flour and gradually add milk and water. Add salt, pepper and cheese and cook, stirring, over low heat until thickened and smooth. Garnish with chopped parsley.

Serves 4 — 6.

Beer-Cheese Soup

Reduce water in above recipe to 1 gill (140 ml) and add ½ pt (275 ml) light ale.

MANHATTAN
CLAM CHOWDER

75 gm .	3 oz	streaky bacon, diced
	1	onion, chopped
450 gm .	1 lb	tinned tomatoes
450 gm .	1 lb	potatoes, peeled and diced
350 gm .	12 oz	minced clams (fresh or tinned)
550 ml .	1 pt	water
	¼ tsp	thyme
	1 tsp	salt
	¼ tsp	pepper

Fry bacon and onion together until crisp and brown. Add remaining ingredients and continue cooking until potatoes are tender. Stir occasionally.

Serves 6.

CORN CHOWDER

50 gm .	2 oz	bacon, diced
	1	onion, chopped
	2 medium	potatoes, peeled and diced
400 ml .	¾ pt	water
425 ml .	¾ pt	milk
		salt
225 gm .	8 oz	tinned sweet corn

Fry bacon and onion together until brown. Drain fat. Add potatoes and water and simmer, covered, until potatoes are tender. Add milk, salt to taste, and corn. Heat to boiling.

Serves 6.

Entrées:

MEAT

POT ROAST OF	*2 kg* . 4-5 lb	lean beef rump
BEEF	1 tbsp	cooking fat or oil
	2 tsp	salt
	⅛ tsp	pepper
	550 ml . 1 pt	water
	12	small whole onions, peeled
	6	carrots, peeled
	1 kg . 2 lb	potatoes, peeled
	4 tbsp	flour
	140 ml . 1 gill	cold water

Brown meat on all sides in hot fat. Sprinkle with salt and pepper and pour water over meat. Bake in covered roasting tin in moderate oven (350°F, 180°C, Gas Mark 4) for 90 minutes. Halve carrots lengthwise and cut into 3-in. (8-cm) pieces; place around meat with onions. Continue cooking 1 hour. Cut potatoes into chunks and add to other vegetables. Cook 30 minutes or until meat and vegetables are tender. Remove meat to large warm platter and place vegetables around it. Make gravy: add flour to cold water and mix until smooth; stir into liquid in roasting tin. Cook over medium heat, stirring, until thickened.
Serves 6 — 8.

STEAK AND	*1 kg* . 2-2½ lb	sirloin steak
MUSHROOMS		salt and pepper
	pinch	garlic powder (optional)
	225 gm . 8 oz	sliced mushrooms
	50 gm . 2 oz	butter

Steak should be 1½ in. thick (4 cm). Cut into four equal pieces. Sprinkle lightly with salt, pepper and garlic powder. Place on grill pan and position under hot grill so that top of steak is 3 in. (8 cm) from heat. Grill 10-12 minutes per side for rare, 15-20 minutes per side for medium. Melt butter in frying pan and fry mushrooms gently until golden-brown and tender. Spoon mushrooms and butter over cooked steaks.
Serves 4.

BRAISED BEEF
TIPS

675 gm .	1½ lb	sirloin steak, cubed
115 gm .	4 oz	sliced mushrooms
50 gm .	2 oz	butter
	1 clove	garlic, crushed
275 ml .	½ pt	water
	1	beef stock cube
	2 tbsp	cornflour
	3 tbsp	cold water

Melt half of butter in large frying pan and fry the mushrooms until tender. Remove mushrooms from pan. Add remaining butter and fry beef cubes until browned on all sides. Add garlic, water and beef cube and simmer 1 hour. Add water to replace liquid which evaporates. Combine cornflour with cold water and stir into liquid. Add mushrooms and cook over low heat, stirring, until thickened.
    Serves 6.

BEEF
STROGANOFF

450 gm (12-mm thick) .		
1 lb (½-in. thick)		beef sirloin
	1 clove	garlic, crushed
	1	onion, minced
50 gm .	2 oz	butter
	3 tbsp	plain flour
	¼ tsp	pepper
274 ml .	½ pt	water
	1	chicken stock cube
170 gm .	6 oz	sliced mushrooms
140 ml .	1 gill	sour cream
	2 tbsp	chopped parsley

Cut meat into small strips. Brown with garlic and onion in melted butter. Stir in flour and pepper. Add water, chicken cube and mushrooms and cook over low heat, stirring frequently, until meat is tender (about 30 minutes). Stir in sour cream and sprinkle with parsley. Serve over rice or noodles.
    Serves 4 — 6.

CHICKEN-FRIED
STEAK

450 gm .	1 lb	lean stewing steak
	1	egg
	1 tbsp	milk
50 gm .	2 oz	plain flour
		salt and pepper
	3 tbsp	cooking fat or oil

Pound steak with meat hammer until it is ¼ in. (6 mm) thick. Cut into serving-size pieces. Beat egg with milk and dip steaks into it. Coat with flour and sprinkle with salt and pepper. Fry in hot fat until brown. Lower heat and cover pan and continue cooking until meat is tender (about 45 minutes). Uncover and cook 5 minutes over high heat to crisp meat.

Serves 4.

BURGUNDY BEEF

125 gm .	4 oz	sliced mushrooms
	3 tbsp	butter
900 gm .	2 lb	lean stewing beef, cubed
	2 tbsp	plain flour
	1 tsp	salt
	¼ tsp	pepper
	¼ tsp	thyme
	¼ tsp	marjoram
	½	bay leaf
550 ml .	1 pt	tomato purée
275 ml .	½ pt	burgundy or other dry red wine

Brown mushrooms in butter and remove from pan. Brown beef in same butter. Sprinkle with flour, salt, pepper, thyme and marjoram and mix well. Add bay leaf, tomato purée and wine. Simmer, covered, 2½ hours. Add mushrooms and simmer 30 minutes.

Serves 6.

SWISS STEAK

900 gm (25-mm thick) . 2 lb (1-in thick)		stewing steak
		salt and pepper
25 gm .	1 oz	plain flour
	3 tbsp	cooking fat or oil
450 gm .	1 lb	tinned tomatoes
	1	onion, chopped
	2 tbsp	plain flour
70 ml .	½ gill	cold water

Cut meat into serving-size pieces and sprinkle lightly with salt and pepper. Pound flour into meat with a meat hammer. Brown meat in hot fat on both sides. Pour off excess fat. Add tomatoes and onion and simmer, covered, until steak is very tender (about 1½ hours). Remove meat to warm platter; mix flour with cold water and stir into sauce. Cook, stirring, until thickened. Spoon sauce over meat.

Serves 4.

BEEF BIRDS

675 gm (12-mm thick) .		
1½ lb (½-in. thick)	stewing steak	
	salt and pepper	
85 gm .	3 oz	breadcrumbs
	1 tsp	salt
	½	onion, minced
	2 tbsp	finely chopped parsley
	2 tbsp	melted butter
	2 tbsp	water
	2 tbsp	cooking fat
275 ml .	½ pt	hot water
	1	beef stock cube
	2 tbsp	cornflour
	3 tbsp	cold water

Sprinkle meat lightly with salt and pepper on both sides. Pound with meat hammer until ¼ in. (6 mm) thick. Cut into four pieces. Combine crumbs, salt, onion, parsley, melted butter and 2 tablespoons water; spread mixture over steaks. Roll up each piece and tie with string. Heat fat in frying pan and brown meat rolls on all sides. Mix hot water and beef cube and pour over meat. Cover and simmer 1 hour. Remove meat to warm platter and remove strings. Mix cornflour with cold water and stir into pan liquid. Cook, stirring, over medium heat until thickened. Add more water if too thick. Spoon gravy over Beef Birds.

Serves 4.

BEEF STEW

900 gm .	2 lb	stewing beef, cubed
85 gm .	3 oz	plain flour
	2 tsp	salt
	½ tsp	pepper
	3 tbsp	cooking fat or oil
	2	onions, sliced
	1	bay leaf
	2 sticks	celery, sliced
	4	carrots, sliced
675 gm .	1½ lb	potatoes, quartered

Mix flour with salt and pepper and coat beef cubes with mixture. Brown on all sides in hot fat. Stir in any remaining flour mixture and add onions, bay leaf and water to cover. Simmer, covered, stirring occasionally, for 2 hours. Add celery, carrots and potatoes and salt and pepper to taste. Simmer until vegetables are tender (about 45 minutes).

Serves 6.

SALISBURY STEAK

450 gm	1 lb	minced raw beef
	¾ tsp	salt
	¼ tsp	pepper
	1 tbsp	minced onion
	2 tbsp	breadcrumbs
	1	egg
	1 tbsp	melted butter

Combine beef, salt, pepper, onion, breadcrumbs and egg and mix thoroughly. Shape into four ovals, about 1 in. (25 mm) thick, and place on grill pan. Brush tops with melted butter and cook under heated grill until browned. Turn meat and brush other side with butter and return to grill until browned and cooked through.

Serves 4.

MEATBALLS

325 gm	12 oz	minced raw beef
	¼	onion, minced
	¾ tsp	salt
	⅛ tsp	pepper
	2 slices	white bread, cubed
70 ml	½ gill	milk
	2 tbsp	cooking fat or oil
	2 tbsp	plain flour
400 ml	¾ pt	water
	½ tsp	salt
	⅛ tsp	pepper

Combine first four ingredients. Mix bread with milk and leave to stand 5 minutes; then stir into meat mixture. Shape into 12 balls and brown in hot fat. Remove from pan. Stir in flour and add water gradually. Add salt and pepper and cook, stirring, until thickened. Return meatballs to gravy and cover. Cook over low heat 30 minutes, stirring occasionally. Serve with rice or noodles or potatoes.

Serves 4.

STUFFED PEPPERS

450 gm	1 lb	minced raw beef
	1 stick	celery, chopped
	½	onion, chopped
	½ tsp	salt
	⅛ tsp	pepper
400 ml	¾ pt	tomato purée
	6 tbsp	water
115 gm	4 oz	quick-cooking rice
	6	green peppers
50 gm	2 oz	Cheddar cheese, grated

Cook beef with celery and onion, stirring until lightly browned. Add salt, pepper, tomato purée and water and simmer 5 minutes. Stir in rice and set aside. Cut tops from peppers and remove seeds. Cook whole peppers 5 minutes in boiling water. Remove and drain. Divide meat filling among peppers and top with grated cheese. Stand them in a baking tin and pour in water to ¼-in. (6-mm) depth. Bake in moderate oven (375° F, 190° C, Gas Mark 5) for 25-30 minutes.

Serves 6.

SPAGHETTI AMERICAN-STYLE		
225 gm . 8 oz	minced raw beef
1	medium onion, chopped
1 tbsp	plain flour
½ tsp	salt
¼ tsp	pepper
½ tsp	oregano
¼ tsp	cinnamon
400 ml . ¾ pt	tomato purée
220 ml . 1½ gills	water
2 tbsp	grated Parmesan cheese
225 gm . 8 oz	spaghetti
	Parmesan cheese for topping

Stir beef and onion over medium heat until browned. Pour off excess fat and stir in flour. Add salt, pepper, oregano, cinnamon, tomato purée, water and Parmesan cheese. Mix well and simmer, uncovered, 1 hour, stirring occasionally. Cook spaghetti in boiling water until tender; drain. Serve sauce over spaghetti and sprinkle with Parmesan.

Serves 4.

PORCUPINE MEATBALLS		
450 gm . 1 lb	minced raw beef
115 gm . 4 oz	long-grain white rice
1	egg
¼	medium-sized onion, minced
¼ tsp	pepper
¼ tsp	salt
200 ml . 1½ gills	tomato purée
140 ml . 1 gill	water

Combine meat, rice, egg, onion, pepper, salt and a quarter of tomato purée; mix well. Shape into 1½-in. (4-cm) balls and place in frying pan. Mix remaining tomato purée with water and pour over meatballs. Simmer, covered, 40 minutes, stirring frequently.

Serves 4 — 6.

HAMBURGER	*900 gm* . 2 lb	potatoes
PIE	2 tbsp	butter
		milk
	450 gm . 1 lb	minced raw beef
	1	small onion, chopped
	1 tsp	salt
	¼ tsp	pepper
	1 tbsp	flour
	275 ml . ½ pt	tomato purée
	275 ml . ½ pt	water
	450 gm . 1 lb	tinned green beans, drained

Boil potatoes in salted water until tender. Drain and mash well, adding the
butter and sufficient milk to make smooth and creamy. Stir beef and onion
with salt and pepper in large frying pan over medium heat until browned.
Stir in flour, add purée, water and beans and continue cooking, stirring,
until mixture bubbles. Pour into ovenproof dish and spoon mashed potatoes in a ring around edge. Bake in a moderate oven (350°F, 180°C, Gas
Mark 4) for 20-25 minutes or until potatoes are lightly browned.
 Serves 6.

BEEF HASH	*340 gm* . 12 oz	cooked minced beef
	1	onion, minced
	2	large cooked potatoes,
		chopped
	1 tsp	salt
	¼ tsp	pepper
	140 ml . 1 gill	milk
	2 tbsp	cooking fat or oil

Combine meat, onion, potatoes, salt, pepper and milk and mix well. Heat oil
in frying pan and spread mixture evenly in hot oil. Fry until brown and crisp
on bottom. Fold in half and lift on to platter.
 Serves 4.

LIVER AND	4 rashers	streaky bacon
BACON	*350 gm* . 12 oz	sliced calves' or beef liver
		flour
		salt and pepper

Fry bacon until crisp and push to sides of frying pan. Coat liver with flour
and sprinkle lightly with salt and pepper. Fry liver in bacon fat, over medium
heat, until brown on both sides. Remove liver to a warm platter and lay
bacon over the top.
 Serves 4.

CALVES' LIVER
IN SOUR CREAM

450 gm .	1 lb	calves' liver, sliced
		flour, salt, pepper
	1½ tbsp	cooking oil
140 ml .	1 gill	sour cream
	¼ tsp	salt
	⅛ tsp	pepper

Coat liver with flour and sprinkle with salt and pepper. Fry in hot oil until brown on both sides. Remove liver and drain on paper towels. Keep warm. Pour off oil and mix sour cream, salt and pepper in frying pan. Heat gently (do not boil), stirring continually, and spoon over liver.
Serves 4.

OVEN-
BARBECUED
SPARERIBS

2¼ kg .	5 lb	lean pork spareribs
		Red Barbecue Sauce
		(see p. 110)

Place ribs in shallow ovenproof baking dish. Bake in a very moderate oven (325°F, 170°C, Gas Mark 3) for 1 hour. Drain off fat and pour sauce over ribs. Continue baking for 30 minutes, basting every 10 minutes with sauce.
Serves 4.

HAM AND
CHEESE
CASSEROLE

50 gm .	2 oz	butter or margarine
50 gm .	2 oz	sliced mushrooms
3½ tbsp .	4 tbsp	flour
375 ml .	¾ pt	milk
150 gm .	6 oz	Cheddar cheese, cubed
	½ tsp	salt
	¼ tsp	pepper
250 gm .	10 oz	cooked ham, cubed
200 gm .	8 oz	cooked potatoes, cubed
	2 tbsp	chopped parsley

Cook mushrooms in butter until tender. Stir in flour. Add milk, cheese, salt and pepper and cook, stirring, until thickened and smooth. Add ham, potatoes and parsley and turn into buttered ovenproof dish. Bake in a moderate oven (375°F, 190°C, Gas Mark 5) for 30 minutes, or until lightly browned.
Serves 6.

WIENER BOATS

450 gm .	1 lb	frankfurter sausages
		mashed potatoes (about
		4 tbsp for each sausage)
50 gm .	2 oz	grated cheese

Split sausages lengthwise, not quite through, and open out. Pile mashed potatoes along centre of each sausage and sprinkle with grated cheese. Place on baking sheet and bake in moderate oven (375°F, 190°C, Gas Mark 5) for 15 minutes.

Serves 4.

LAMB STEW			
	450 gm .	1 lb	boneless lamb cubes
		1 tsp	salt
		⅛ tsp	pepper
		3 tbsp	plain flour
	400 ml .	¾ pt	water
		2	onions, sliced
		2	carrots, peeled and sliced
		2	potatoes, cubed
	200 gm .	8 oz	frozen peas

Brown lamb cubes on all sides (if meat is very lean use small amount of fat or oil). Sprinkle with salt, pepper and flour and stir until flour is absorbed. Add water gradually, stirring until mixture thickens. Add onions and carrots, cover, and simmer gently one hour, stirring occasionally. Add potatoes and continue cooking 20 minutes. Add peas and cook 10 minutes longer. Add additional salt and pepper if necessary.

Serves 4.

POULTRY

CHICKEN AND DUMPLINGS			
	2 kg .	4-5 lb	chicken, cut up
	75 gm .	3 oz	fat or oil
	550 ml .	1 pt	water
		1 tsp	salt
		¼ tsp	pepper
		pinch	thyme
		4 tbsp	plain flour
	275 ml .	½ pt	milk
			Dumplings

Fry chicken in hot fat until browned on both sides. Remove chicken and pour off fat, setting aside 3 tablespoons. Return chicken to frying pan, add water, salt, pepper and thyme. Simmer, covered, until chicken is tender (2-3 hours). Remove chicken pieces to an ovenproof dish and pour liquid into a basin; skim fat from liquid. Melt the 3 tablespoons fat and stir in flour. Add cooking liquid and milk gradually; cook, stirring, until thickened. Season with salt and pepper to taste. Pour over the chicken. Prepare mixture for Dumplings and drop by spoonfuls on to hot chicken and gravy. Cover and bake 30 minutes in a very moderate oven (325°F, 170°C, Gas Mark 3).

Serves 6 — 8.

Dumplings	*170 gm* . 6 oz	plain flour
	2 tsp	baking powder
	¼ tsp	salt
	4 tbsp	milk or buttermilk
	3 tbsp	salad oil

Mix dry ingredients. Mix milk with oil and stir into flour mixture. Drop by tablespoons onto hot stew.

Savoury Dumplings

Add 2 tbsp chopped parsley, ¼ tsp thyme, ¼ tsp sage, and ¼ tsp pepper to flour mixture in above recipe.

OVEN-	*1¼ kg* . 3 lb	frying chicken, cut into joints
BARBECUED	*25 gm* . 1 oz	fat or oil for frying
CHICKEN		Red Barbecue Sauce (see p. 110)

Melt fat in large frying pan and fry chicken on both sides until medium brown. Remove to ovenproof dish. Pour Barbecue Sauce over chicken and bake in a very moderate oven (325°F, 170°C, Gas Mark 3) for 45 minutes, basting every 15 minutes.

Serves 4.

STEWED	*1½-2½ kg* . 3-5 lb	chicken
CHICKEN	*800 ml* . 1½ pt	water
	1 tsp	salt

Place chicken in large saucepan and add water and salt. Bring to boil, lower heat and cover tightly. Simmer gently until tender (1-3 hours, depending on size and age of bird). Remove bird to platter and strain broth. Cool. Remove bones and skin from chicken. Skim fat from broth.

Chicken may be used in any recipe calling for cooked boneless chicken. Use broth for soup or any recipe calling for chicken broth.

Yield: about 1 lb (450 gm) cooked boneless chicken.

CHICKEN DIVAN

1¼ kg . 3 lb	chicken breasts
2 tsp	salt
450 gm . 1 lb	broccoli
4 tbsp	butter
4 tbsp	plain flour
550 ml . 1 pt	milk
½ tsp	salt
dash	pepper
100 gm . 4 oz	Cheddar cheese, cubed .

Place chicken breasts in water to cover. Add salt and bring to boil. Simmer, covered, until tender. Remove skin and bones and cut chicken into slices. Trim broccoli and cut into 4-in. (10-cm) stalks. Cook just until tender, in boiling water. Melt butter and add flour. Stir in milk, add salt, pepper and cheese and cook, stirring, over medium heat until thickened and smooth. Arrange half of the chicken in a shallow ovenproof dish. Top with broccoli and then remaining chicken slices. Pour sauce over all. Bake in a moderate oven (375°F, 190°C, Gas Mark 5) for 30 minutes.

Serves 6.

CHICKEN À LA KING

50 gm . 2 oz	butter
8 large	mushrooms, sliced
½	green pepper, chopped
50 gm . 2 oz	plain flour
1 tsp	salt
¼ tsp	pepper
500 ml . 1 pt	milk
300 gm . 12 oz	cooked boneless chicken, cubed
1 small	pimento, chopped
	toast

Melt butter and fry mushrooms and green pepper until tender. Stir in flour, salt and pepper; add milk gradually. Cook, stirring, until thickened. Add chicken and stir gently until heated through. Stir in pimento and serve immediately over toast.

Serves 6.

CHICKEN LIVERS IN MUSHROOM-WINE SAUCE	450 gm . 1 lb	chicken livers, cut up
	¼	onion, chopped
	3 tbsp	butter or margarine
	1 tsp	salt
	¼ tsp	pepper
	3 tbsp	plain flour
	140 ml . 1 gill	water
	140 ml . 1 gill	dry red wine
	50-gm tin . 2 oz tin	chopped mushrooms, drained

Fry livers and onion in butter, stirring, until brown. Stir in salt, pepper and flour and gradually add water and wine. Add mushrooms and simmer gently, stirring frequently, for 20 minutes. Serve over rice.

Serves 4.

CURRIED CHICKEN LIVERS	450 gm . 1 lb	chicken livers
	1	small onion, chopped
	4	mushrooms, sliced
	4 tbsp	butter
	4 tbsp	plain flour
	2 tbsp	curry powder
	1 tsp	salt
	400 ml . ¾ pt	water

Fry chicken livers, onion and mushrooms in butter until browned. Stir in flour, curry and salt. Add water gradually; simmer 10 minutes, stirring frequently. Serve with rice.

Serves 4.

MISCELLANEOUS

YORK STATE BAKED BEANS	400 gm . 1 lb	dried haricot beans
	100 gm . 4 oz	streaky bacon, diced
	1	onion, chopped
	50 gm . 2 oz	brown sugar
	1 tsp	salt
	250 ml . ½ pt	tomato purée

Soak beans in cold water overnight. Drain and cover with fresh water. Bring to boil and simmer 30 minutes. Drain, saving liquid. Mix beans, onion and bacon in deep ovenproof dish. Combine brown sugar, salt and tomato purée with 1 pint bean liquid. Pour over beans and add more bean liquid until beans are covered. Cover dish and bake in a very slow oven (275°F, 135°C, Gas Mark 1) for 3 hours, or until tender, adding more liquid if necessary. Uncover and bake 30 minutes.

Serves 8.

MACARONI	100 gm . 4 oz	short macaroni pieces
AND	5 tsp . 2 tbsp	butter or margarine
CHEESE	5 tsp . 2 tbsp	plain flour
	375 ml . ¾ pt	milk
	¾ tsp	salt
	⅛ tsp	pepper
	150 gm . 6 oz	Cheddar cheese, cubed

Cook macaroni in boiling salt water until barely tender. Drain. Melt butter and blend in flour. Stir in milk, add salt, pepper and cheese, and cook over low heat, stirring, until thickened and smooth. Add macaroni and turn into buttered ovenproof dish. Bake in moderate oven (375°F, 190°C, Gas Mark 5) for 30 minutes or until browned on top.

Serves 4.

Vegetables

**POTATO-SOUR-
CREAM
CASSEROLE**

1 l.	1 qt	mashed potatoes
125 ml.	1 gill	sour cream
		salt, pepper
100 gm.	4 oz	sliced mushrooms
2½ tbsp.	3 tbsp	butter
	2	spring onions, chopped
	2 tbsp	chopped parsley
	3 tbsp	butter

Combine potatoes, sour cream and salt and pepper to taste. Spread half of mixture in a greased ovenproof dish. Fry mushrooms in 3 tablespoons butter until tender and spread over potatoes. Sprinkle onions and parsley over and cover with remaining mashed potatoes. Dot with 3 tablespoons butter and bake in moderate oven (375°F, 190°C, Gas Mark 5) until golden-brown (about 30 minutes).
Serves 6.

**BAKED
POTATOES DE
LUXE**

	4	large potatoes
		salt, pepper
140 ml.	1 gill	sour cream
	2 tbsp	finely chopped chives
	2 rashers	streaky bacon, cooked until crisp, and crumbled

Scrub potatoes and pierce in several places with point of small knife. Rub skins lightly with oil. Bake in a moderately hot oven (400°F, 200°C, Gas Mark 6) for 1 hour, or until tender. Cut a cross in the top of each potato and press sides until it opens up. Sprinkle lightly with salt and pepper and top with generous amounts of sour cream. Sprinkle chives and bacon bits over top.
Serves 4.

**BAKED STUFFED
POTATOES**

	4	large baking potatoes
	4 tbsp	butter
	¾ tsp	salt
	⅛ tsp	pepper
100 ml (approx).	½-1 gill	milk
50 gm.	2 oz	Cheddar cheese, grated

Scrub potatoes and puncture them in several places with small sharp knife. Bake in a moderately hot oven (400°F, 200°C, Gas Mark 6) until tender (about 1 hour). Cut potatoes in halves, scoop out insides and mash well with butter, salt, pepper and enough milk to give smooth, fluffy texture. Pile potato mixture back into skins and top with grated cheese. Bake in moderate oven (350°F, 180°C, Gas Mark 4) 30 minutes.

Serves 8.

PARSLEY POTATOES	675 gm . 1½ lb	small new potatoes
	550 ml . 1 pt	water
	2 tsp	salt
	2 tbsp	melted butter
	2 tbsp	chopped parsley

Scrub or scrape potatoes and cut into halves. Add water and salt and bring to boil. Simmer, covered, until tender. Drain. Add parsley to melted butter and pour over potatoes.

Serves 4.

CREAMED NEW POTATOES AND PEAS	900 gm . 2 lb	new potatoes
	225 gm . 8 oz	shelled fresh peas or frozen peas
	4 tbsp	butter
	4 tbsp	plain flour
	550 ml . 1 pt	milk
	½ tsp	salt
	dash	pepper

Scrape potatoes, cut into cubes and place in saucepan. Cover with water, add 1 teaspoon salt, and simmer, covered, 10 minutes. Add peas and return to boil. Simmer until potatoes are tender (5-10 minutes). Drain and turn into serving dish. Melt butter and stir in flour. Gradually add milk, salt and pepper and cook, stirring, over medium heat until thick. Pour over the potatoes and peas.

Serves 6.

CAULIFLOWER AU GRATIN	900 gm . 2 lb	cauliflower
	4 tbsp	butter
	5 tbsp	plain flour
	360 ml . ⅔ pt	milk
	¾ tsp	salt
	¼ tsp	pepper
	75 gm . 3 oz	Cheddar cheese, cubed

Remove leaves and break cauliflower into small pieces. Place in saucepan with 1 pt (550 ml) water and 1 teaspoon salt and heat to boiling. Simmer, covered, 10 minutes. Drain and turn into buttered ovenproof dish. Melt butter, stir in flour and gradually add milk, salt, pepper and cheese. Cook over medium heat, stirring, until mixture thickens and cheese has melted. Pour over cauliflower and bake in a moderate oven (350°F, 180°C, Gas Mark 4) for 30 minutes.

Serves 4 — 6.

Potatoes Au Gratin

In place of cauliflower in above recipe use 2 lb (900 gm) potatoes, peeled, cut into chunks and cooked until barely tender. Proceed according to recipe.

SCALLOPED CORN

	4 tbsp	butter
	2 tbsp	plain flour
275 ml .	½ pt	milk
	½ tsp	salt
	⅛ tsp	pepper
450 gm .	1 lb	tinned sweet corn, drained
	1	egg, beaten
75 gm .	3 oz	dry breadcrumbs

Melt 3 tablespoons of butter, stir in flour and gradually add milk. Cook over low heat, stirring, until thickened. Add salt, pepper and drained corn and mix well. Add beaten egg and three-quarters of the crumbs and turn into a buttered ovenproof dish. Sprinkle remaining crumbs over surface and dot with remaining butter. Bake in moderate oven (350°F, 180°C, Gas Mark 4) for 20 minutes.

Serves 4.

FIESTA CORN

450 gm .	1 lb	tinned sweet corn
	1 stick	celery, chopped
	1	spring onion, chopped
	¼	green pepper, chopped
	1	pimento, chopped
	½ tsp	salt
	½ tsp	chilli powder
	1 tbsp	butter

Combine corn and its liquid with celery, onion, green pepper, pimento, salt and chilli powder. Simmer, covered, 5 minutes. Drain and add butter.
Serves 4 — 6.

SAVOURY CARROTS

350 gm .	12 oz	carrots
	2	beef stock cubes
275 ml .	½ pt	water
	¼ tsp	ginger
	¼ tsp	marjoram
	2 tbsp	melted butter
	1 tbsp	chopped parsley

Peel and slice carrots. Place in saucepan with beef cubes, water, ginger and marjoram and simmer, covered, until tender. Drain and turn into serving dish. Pour melted butter over and sprinkle with parsley.

COURGETTES MEDLEY

450 gm .	1 lb	small courgettes
	1 rasher	streaky bacon, chopped
	½	onion, chopped
	1 stick	celery, chopped
	2 small	tomatoes, chopped
	¼ tsp	salt
	⅛ tsp	pepper
	¼ tsp	marjoram

Peel and slice courgettes. Cook bacon 2 minutes. Combine all ingredients in covered saucepan and cook over medium heat, stirring occasionally, 10 minutes.
Serves 4 — 6.

BAKED STUFFED COURGETTES

900 gm .	2 lb	courgettes, whole
	4 tbsp	butter
	2	eggs
55 gm .	2 oz	fine breadcrumbs
40 gm .	1½ oz	grated cheese
	1 small	onion, minced
	2 tbsp	chopped parsley
	½ tsp	salt
	⅛ tsp	pepper
	¼ tsp	marjoram

Drop courgettes into boiling water. Return to boil and cook 10 minutes. Remove and cool. Cut in halves lengthwise and scoop out pulp leaving ¼-in. (6-mm) shell. Mash pulp with remaining ingredients and pile into shells. Bake in a moderate oven (350°F, 180°C, Gas Mark 4) 30 minutes.

Serves 6.

PEAS WITH MUSHROOMS

50 gm	2 oz	sliced mushrooms
	2 tbsp	butter
250 gm	10 oz	frozen peas
125 ml	1 gill	water
	½ tsp	salt

Fry mushrooms gently in butter until tender. Add peas, water and salt and simmer, covered, 8 minutes. Drain.

Serves 4 — 6.

GREEN BEANS WITH BACON

350 gm fresh or	12 oz fresh or	
400 gm tinned	1 lb tinned	green beans
25 gm	1 oz	streaky bacon, diced
	¼	onion, diced

Wash and trim fresh beans and cut into short lengths. Cook in boiling salted water until tender (about 20 minutes). Cook bacon and onion together until tender and add to cooked beans and liquid (or tinned beans with liquid). Simmer 5 minutes. Drain.

Serves 4.

CREAMED SPINACH

900 gm	2 lb	fresh spinach
	2 tbsp	minced onion
	2 tbsp	butter
	2 tbsp	plain flour
140 ml	1 gill	milk
	¼ tsp	nutmeg
	½ tsp	salt
	⅛ tsp	pepper

Wash spinach thoroughly and cook in small amount of water until barely tender. Drain and press out all liquid. Chop. Fry onion in butter until tender. Stir in flour and add milk gradually. Add nutmeg, salt, pepper and spinach and cook, stirring gently, over low heat until sauce is thickened.

Serves 6.

Sauces

WHITE SAUCE

	2 tbsp	butter or margarine
	2 tbsp	plain flour
275 ml .	½ pt	milk
	¼ tsp	salt

Melt butter and stir in flour. Gradually add milk and salt and stir over low heat until mixture is thickened. Use as basis for creamed dishes, or as sauce for vegetables or fish.

Parsley Sauce

Prepare White Sauce. Stir in 1 tablespoon chopped parsley.

CHEESE SAUCE

	3 tbsp	butter or margarine
	3 tbsp	plain flour
400 ml .	¾ pt	milk
75 gm .	3 oz	Cheddar cheese, cubed
	½ tsp	salt
	dash	pepper

Melt butter and stir in flour. Add milk gradually. Add cheese, salt and pepper; cook, stirring, until cheese has melted and sauce is thickened and smooth.

TOMATO SAUCE

	2 tbsp	butter or margarine
	½	onion, chopped
	2 tbsp	plain flour
275 ml .	½ pt	tomato juice
	⅛ tsp	pepper
	½ tsp	brown sugar
	½	bay leaf
	2	whole cloves

Fry onion in butter until tender. Stir in flour and add tomato juice gradually. Add pepper, brown sugar, bay leaf, cloves and simmer, uncovered, 30 minutes, stirring frequently. Strain. Serve with meat or fish.

Salads and Salad Dressings

COLESLAW   *225 gm* . 8 oz   crisp raw cabbage
         4 tbsp   mayonnaise
         1 tbsp   lemon juice
         ¼ tsp   salt
         1 tbsp   honey or sugar
         1 stick   celery, chopped
                 (optional)

Shred or chop cabbage until very fine. Mix with chopped celery, if used. Combine mayonnaise with lemon juice, salt and honey and pour over cabbage. Mix well. Chill.

    Serves 6.

Apple-Raisin Slaw

Add half a cooking apple, peeled, cored and diced, and 1 oz (25 gm) raisins.

Pineapple Slaw

Add one small tin crushed pineapple, undrained. Omit lemon juice.

TOSSED GARDEN SALAD   ½ head   crisp lettuce, torn
                             into small pieces
         1 large   tomato, chopped
         1   spring onion, chopped
         ½ stick   celery, chopped
         1 sprig   parsley, chopped
         ¼   green pepper, chopped

Combine all ingredients in salad bowl. Just before serving, toss lightly with salad dressing.

CARROT-RAISIN
SALAD

	4 large	carrots, grated
75 gm .	3 oz	raisins
	1 stick	celery, chopped
	6 tbsp	mayonnaise
	1 tbsp	lemon juice
	2 tsp	sugar

Combine carrots, raisins and celery. Mix remaining ingredients and pour over vegetables; mix well. Chill 1-2 hours.

Serves 4.

SPINACH AND
EGG SALAD

450 gm .	1 lb	raw spinach
	½	medium-sized onion, chopped
	2	hard-boiled eggs, diced
		Italian Dressing

Wash spinach and pat dry on paper towels. Tear into small pieces. Combine with onion and egg. Chill. Just before serving, pour Italian Dressing over salad and toss lightly.

Serves 6.

ITALIAN
DRESSING

70 ml .	½ gill	salad oil
	3 tbsp	vinegar
	½ tsp	salt
	⅛ tsp	pepper
	⅛ tsp	garlic powder
	⅛ tsp	basil
	⅛ tsp	marjoram
	⅛ tsp	oregano
	⅛ tsp	mustard powder
	dash	cayenne pepper

Mix ingredients in jar or bottle. Cover tightly and shake well. Chill. Shake again before using.

MARINATED
TOMATOES

	2 large	firm ripe tomatoes
140 ml .	1 gill	Italian Dressing

Cut tomatoes into thick slices and place in large shallow dish. Pour dressing over, cover dish, and refrigerate two hours.

Serves 4.

Marinated Cucumbers

Substitute one large cucumber, peeled and sliced, for tomatoes.

ZUCCHINI-	*250 gm* .	8-10 oz	courgettes, thinly sliced
APPLE		1	large cooking apple, cored
SALAD			and diced
		2	spring onions, chopped
		½	green pepper, slivered
	70 ml .	½ gill	salad oil
		2 tsp	lemon juice
		1 tbsp	vinegar
		½ tsp	sugar
		½ tsp	basil
		½ tsp	salt
		⅛ tsp	pepper

Combine courgettes, apple, onions, and green pepper in salad bowl. Mix remaining ingredients thoroughly and pour over. Toss lightly, cover and chill 3 hours. Toss again before serving.

Serves 4 — 6.

SAUERKRAUT			
SALAD	*450-gm jar* .	1-lb jar	sauerkraut
		1	green pepper, chopped
		1	medium-sized onion, chopped
		2 sticks	celery, chopped
		2	pimentos, chopped
	140 ml .	1 gill	vinegar
	70 ml .	½ gill	salad oil
		½ tsp	pepper
	75 gm .	3 oz	sugar
		1 tsp	salt

Drain sauerkraut, rinse with cold water and drain again. Add green pepper, onion, celery and pimento. Mix remaining ingredients and bring to boil. Simmer 2 minutes, stirring. Cool slightly and pour over sauerkraut mixture. Chill several hours.

Serves 6 — 8.

CUCUMBERS IN		1 large	cucumber
SOUR CREAM	*140 ml* .	1 gill	sour cream
		1 tsp	sugar

¾ tsp	salt
2 tsp	vinegar
2 tsp	lemon juice
⅛ tsp	pepper

Slice cucumber. Mix remaining ingredients thoroughly and pour over. Mix gently and chill 1 hour.

Serves 4 — 6.

FRUIT SALAD

225 gm .	8 oz	tinned mandarin oranges, drained
	1 tbsp	juice from oranges
	1	apple, peeled and chopped
	1	banana, sliced
	1½ tbsp	mayonnaise

Mix juice from oranges with mayonnaise. Combine fruits and add mayonnaise mixture. Mix well and chill at least 1 hour.

Serves 4.

FIVE CUP SALAD

1 cup*	pineapple chunks
1 cup	mandarin oranges
1 cup	desiccated coconut
1 cup	sour cream
1 cup	miniature marshmallows

*Use any container as a 'cup'. e.g. a small teacup for a salad to serve 4 — 6; a pint or half-litre measure to serve a large group.

Drain pineapple and oranges. Combine with other ingredients and mix thoroughly. Chill several hours or overnight.

WALDORF SALAD

	2	red apples
	2 sticks	celery, chopped
50 gm .	2 oz	walnut pieces
	4 tbsp	mayonnaise
	1 tbsp	sugar
	½ tsp	salt
	1 tsp	lemon juice
140 ml .	1 gill	thick cream, whipped
	6	dates, stoned and chopped (optional)

Core and dice apples but do not peel. Combine with celery, nuts and dates.
Mix mayonnaise with sugar, salt and lemon juice. Blend in whipped cream.
Fold into apple mixture. Chill.

Serves 6.

PERFECTION	1 tbsp	unflavoured gelatine
SALAD	*50 gm* . 2 oz	sugar
	¼ tsp	salt
	225 gm . 8 oz	tinned crushed pineapple, with juice
	3 tbsp	lemon juice
	50 gm . 2 oz	finely shredded raw cabbage
	½ stick	celery, finely chopped
	2 tbsp	chopped green pepper
	10	stuffed green olives, sliced

Dissolve gelatine, sugar and salt in ⅓ pt (180 ml) boiling water. Drain pineapple and add 3 tablespoons of the juice, the lemon juice, pineapple, and ½
pt (275 ml) cold water. Mix well and chill until partially set. Stir in vegetables
and pour into a mould. Chill until firm. Unmould onto lettuce leaves.

Serves 4.

PINEAPPLE-	1 packet	lime-flavour jelly
CHEESE SALAD	*275 ml* . ½ pt	boiling water
MOULD	*450 gm* . 1 lb	tinned crushed pineapple, with juice
	225 gm . 8 oz	cottage cheese

Dissolve jelly in boiling water. Add pineapple, juice, and cottage cheese, and
pour into a liquidizer. Blend 30 seconds. Pour into a mould and chill until
set. Unmould onto a plate just before serving.

SUNSHINE	1 packet	lemon-flavour jelly
SALAD	*275 ml* . ½ pt	boiling water
	225 gm . 8 oz	tinned crushed pineapple
	½ tsp	salt
	2	carrots, peeled and grated

Pour boiling water over jelly and stir until dissolved. Drain pineapple and
measure juice. Add cold water to make 1 gill (140 ml) and combine with jelly,
pineapple and salt. Mix well and chill until thick but not set. Stir in carrots
and pour into a mould. Chill until set.

Serves 6.

TOMATO ASPIC

1½ tbsp	unflavoured gelatine
275 ml . ½ pt	boiling water
¼ tsp	salt
¼ tsp	pepper
1	beef stock cube
400 ml . ¾ pt	tomato juice
1 tbsp	lemon juice
1 tsp	Worcestershire sauce
2	spring onions, chopped
2 sticks	celery, finely chopped
½	green pepper, finely chopped
¼	cucumber, chopped

Mix gelatine with boiling water, salt, pepper and beef cube in small saucepan. Stir over low heat until dissolved. Combine with tomato juice, lemon juice and Worcestershire sauce. Chill until syrupy but not set. Stir in raw vegetables and pour into a mould. Chill until set (3-4 hours) and unmould onto a plate.

Serves 8 — 10.

MAYONNAISE

1	egg
2 tbsp	lemon juice or vinegar
1 tsp	salt
½ tsp	mustard powder
4 tbsp	salad oil
180 ml . ⅓ pt	salad oil

Place first five ingredients in liquidizer and blend 5 seconds. With liquidizer running, pour in additional salad oil slowly. Turn off immediately.

LUNCHEON SALADS

CHICKEN SALAD

450 gm . 1 lb	cooked boneless chicken
4 sticks	celery
½ tsp	salt
⅛ tsp	pepper
140 ml . 1 gill	mayonnaise
	lettuce leaves
3	hard-boiled eggs, sliced
3	tomatoes, cut into eighths

Chop chicken and celery very fine and mix well with salt, pepper and mayonnaise. Chill mixture well. Arrange lettuce leaves on individual salad plates and place a mound of chicken mixture in centre of each. Arrange tomato wedges and sliced hard-boiled eggs around chicken.

Serves 4 — 6.

TUNA SALAD

175 gm . 6 oz	tinned tuna, drained and flaked
1	spring onion, chopped
½ stick	celery, chopped
1	hard-boiled egg, chopped
⅛ tsp	pepper
¼ tsp	salt
2 tsp	lemon juice
3 tbsp	mayonnaise

Combine all ingredients and mix lightly. Cover and chill. Serve on lettuce leaves.

Serves 6.

STUFFED TOMATOES

4 large	firm, ripe tomatoes
	lettuce leaves
	salt and pepper
	Tuna Salad or Chicken Salad
	parsley sprigs

Cut each tomato into eight sections but leave joined at bottom. Arrange 2 or 3 lettuce leaves on each of four salad plates and place tomatoes in centres. Pull sections open and sprinkle lightly with salt and pepper. Fill centres with Tuna Salad or Chicken Salad and garnish with parsley.

Serves 4.

CHEF'S SALAD

1 small	head lettuce, shredded
125 gm . 4 oz	sliced cooked ham
100 gm . 4 oz	sliced cheese
4	hard-boiled eggs, quartered
4	tomatoes, cut into wedges
12	black olives, stoned

Arrange shredded lettuce on four individual salad plates. Cut ham and cheese into thin strips and place over lettuce. Arrange eggs, tomatoes and olives around. Serve with Chef's Dressing, or any preferred salad dressing.

Serves 6.

CHEF'S	140 ml .	1 gill	salad oil
DRESSING	70 ml .	½ gill	vinegar
		2 tbsp	lemon juice
		1 tbsp	grated onion
		1 tsp	salt
		½ tsp	pepper
		⅛ tsp	tarragon
		1 tbsp	sugar

Place all ingredients in jar and cover tightly. Shake well and chill. Shake again before serving.

EGG SALAD	6	hard-boiled eggs, chopped
	1 stick	celery, chopped
	½	green pepper, chopped
	1	spring onion, chopped
	½ tsp	salt
	⅛ tsp	pepper
	4 tbsp	mayonnaise

Combine all ingredients and mix lightly. Chill. Serve on lettuce leaves with tomato wedges.
   Serves 4.

Desserts and Puddings

CHEESECAKE

Crust

75 gm	3 oz	sweetmeal biscuits, finely crushed
5 tsp	2 tbsp	sugar
2½ tbsp	3 tbsp	melted butter

Filling

400 gm	1 lb	cream cheese
65 ml	½ gill	thick cream
	3	eggs
125 gm	5 oz	sugar
	½ tsp	vanilla essence
1¾ tsp	2 tsp	lemon juice

Combine crushed biscuits, sugar and melted butter for crust. Press firmly into bottom and sides of a 9-in. (23-cm) flan ring. Chill.

Beat cream cheese and cream together until smooth. Beat in eggs, one at a time. Add sugar and mix well. Stir in vanilla and lemon juice. Pour into chilled crust and bake in a moderate oven (350°F, 180°C, Gas Mark 4) until set (about 45-50 minutes). Keep at room temperature until completely cold. Refrigerate.

Serves 8.

LEMON ANGEL PIES

Meringue Crusts

	2	egg whites
	pinch	salt
100 gm	4 oz	sugar
	¼ tsp	vinegar
	½ tsp	vanilla essence

Filling

	3	egg yolks
100 gm	4 oz	sugar
	¼ tsp	salt
2½ tbsp	3 tbsp	cornflour
250 ml	½ pt	water
	1	lemon (juice and grated rind)

Topping

250 ml	½ pt	double cream
	2 tbsp	sugar

Beat egg whites and salt until stiff. Add sugar, 1 tablespoon at a time, beating well. Add vinegar and vanilla and beat 5 minutes longer. Spoon into six circles on a buttered baking sheet, making a depression in the centre of each to form a nest. Bake in a very slow oven (275° F, 135° C, Gas Mark 1) for 45 minutes. Turn off heat and leave in oven 20 minutes. Cool.

Prepare Filling: Mix egg yolks, sugar, salt and cornflour. Gradually add water, lemon juice and rind, and cook, stirring, over low heat until thickened. Cool. Spoon into cooled meringue crusts. Beat cream and sugar for Topping together until stiff. Spoon over filling.

Serves 6.

GLORIFIED RICE

150 gm .	6 oz	cooked white rice
50 gm .	2 oz	sugar
200 gm .	8 oz	tinned crushed pineapple
50 gm .	2 oz	miniature marshmallows
	8	maraschino cherries, chopped
250 ml .	½ pt	thick cream, whipped

Combine rice, sugar and pineapple. Stir in marshmallows and cherries and mix lightly with whipped cream. Chill several hours.

Serves 6 — 8.

RICE-RAISIN PUDDING

100 gm .	4 oz	sugar
100 gm .	4 oz	cooked white rice
	½ tsp	cinnamon
	½ tsp	nutmeg
	¼ tsp	salt
50 gm .	2 oz	raisins
	2	eggs, beaten
500 ml .	1 pt	milk

Mix sugar, rice, cinnamon, nutmeg, salt and raisins. Add eggs and mix well. Stir in milk gradually. Pour into buttered ovenproof dish and place in a cold oven. Turn heat to 350° F (180° C, Gas Mark 4) and bake 45 minutes, stirring after 20 minutes.

BREAD PUDDING

	2	eggs, beaten
75 gm .	3 oz	sugar
500 ml .	1 pt	milk
100 gm .	4 oz	soft bread cubes
	½ tsp	cinnamon
	½ tsp	nutmeg
50 gm .	2 oz	raisins

Combine eggs with sugar. Heat milk almost to boiling. Mix bread cubes, cinnamon, nutmeg and raisins and pour hot milk over them. Mix well. Add small amount of hot mixture to egg-sugar mixture, then stir back into bread mixture. Pour into buttered ovenproof dish. Set dish in slightly larger baking tin of hot water and bake in moderate oven (350° F, 180° C, Gas Mark 4) for 50-60 minutes, or until set. Serve warm or cold.

Serves 4 — 6.

BAKED APPLE PUDDING	100 gm . 4 oz	plain flour
	125 gm . 5 oz	sugar
	1 tsp	bicarbonate of soda
	½ tsp	salt
	1 tsp	cinnamon
	½ tsp	ginger
	¼ tsp	cloves
	¼ tsp	nutmeg
	1	egg
	1 tsp	vanilla essence
	400 gm . 1 lb	applesauce
	50 gm . 2 oz	raisins

Mix flour, sugar, soda, salt and spices. Stir in egg, vanilla and applesauce and mix well. Add raisins and pour into buttered 9-in. (23-cm) square baking tin. Bake in a moderate oven (350° F, 180° C, Gas Mark 4) for 45 minutes. Serve warm with cream or ice cream.

Serves 8 — 10.

BAKED APPLES	4 large	apples
	25 gm . 1 oz	raisins
	75 gm . 3 oz	brown sugar
	25 gm . 1 oz	butter

Core apples but do not peel. Stand upright in a baking tin. Mix raisins, brown sugar and butter together and fill apple centres with mixture. Pour water into tin to depth of ¼ in. (6 mm) and bake in a very moderate oven (325° F, 170° C, Gas Mark 3) until tender (about 45 minutes). Serve warm or cold.

STRAWBERRY SHORTCAKE	400 gm . 1 lb	fresh strawberries
	50 gm . 2 oz	sugar
	4	Shortcakes, split
		whipped cream

Remove stems from strawberries and slice them. Mix with sugar and allow to stand until juicy. Place bottom half of Shortcake on each of four dessert plates. Spoon half of berries and juice over them. Replace tops of Shortcakes and spoon remaining berries and juice over them. Top with generous amount of whipped cream.

Serves 4.

Shortcakes	100 gm .	4 oz	plain flour
		1 tsp	baking powder
		¼ tsp	salt
	2½ tbsp .	3 tbsp	cooking fat
		1	egg yolk
	3½ tbsp .	4 tbsp	milk

Sieve flour, baking powder and salt and rub in fat. Beat egg yolk and mix with milk. Add to flour mixture and mix well. Roll out to ¼-in. (6-mm) thickness on lightly floured board and cut into rounds. Bake in a moderate oven (350° F, 180°C, Gas Mark 4) until lightly browned (about 20 minutes).

QUICK STRAWBERRY SHORTCAKES

plain cake squares or spongecakes
frozen sweetened strawberries, thawed
sweetened whipped cream or ice cream

Split cake squares or spongecakes and spoon berries over them. Top with whipped cream or ice cream.

VANILLA PUDDING	3 tbsp .	3½ tbsp	cornflour
		¼ tsp	salt
	75 gm .	3 oz	sugar
	500 ml .	1 pt	milk
	2½ tbsp .	3 tbsp	butter
		½ tsp	vanilla essence

Mix cornflour, salt and sugar and gradually add milk. Cook over low heat, stirring, until thickened. Add butter and vanilla and pour into a mould or basin. Chill.

Serves 4.

Butterscotch Pudding

Prepare as for Vanilla Pudding but use 4 oz (100 gm) brown sugar in place of granulated sugar.

CHOCOLATE PUDDING

50 gm	2 oz	semi-sweet chocolate
25 gm	1 oz	butter
4 tbsp	4½ tbsp	cornflour
100 gm	4 oz	sugar
	¼ tsp	salt
500 ml	1 pt	milk
	1 tsp	vanilla essence

Melt chocolate and butter together in top of double saucepan over hot water. Mix cornflour, sugar and salt and gradually stir in milk. Combine with melted chocolate and butter and cook over low heat, stirring, until mixture is thickened. Stir in vanilla. Cool.
Serves 4.

CHOCOLATE FONDUE

200 gm	8 oz	semi-sweet chocolate
3½ tbsp	4 tbsp	sugar
125 ml	1 gill	evaporated milk
1 tsp	1 tsp	vanilla essence
2½ tsp	1 tbsp	butter
		cake cubes
		banana chunks
		large marshmallows
		cherries
		strawberries
		pineapple chunks

Heat chocolate, sugar, milk, vanilla and butter in fondue pot over low heat, stirring until smooth. Serve in the fondue pot and provide each person with a long-handled fondue fork for spearing and dipping cake, fruit, etc.
Serves 4 — 6.

LEMON SNOW PUDDING

2½ tbsp	3 tbsp	cornflour
	¼ tsp	salt
100 gm	4 oz	sugar
	3	egg yolks
250 ml	½ pt	water
	1	lemon (juice and grated rind)
	3	egg whites

Mix cornflour, salt, sugar and egg yolks. Gradually add water, lemon juice and rind. Cook, stirring, over low heat until thickened. Cool slightly. Beat egg whites until stiff. Fold in lemon mixture. Pour into dish and chill.
   Serves 6.

FLOATING ISLAND

2 tbsp .	2½ tbsp	cornflour
75 gm .	3 oz	sugar
	2	eggs, separated
500 ml .	1 pt	milk
	⅛ tsp	salt

Combine cornflour, *half* of sugar, and egg yolks. Gradually add milk. Cook in top of double saucepan over hot water until thickened. Pour into large glass dish and chill. Beat egg whites with salt until stiff. Add remaining sugar a little at a time, beating well after each addition. Drop meringue by large spoonfuls into simmering water and poach 2-3 minutes. Lift with slotted spoon and place islands of meringue on top of custard.
   Serves 6.

CHOCOLATE ICE BOX CAKE

150 gm .	6 oz	sponge cakes
375 ml .	¾ pt	milk
50 gm .	2 oz	semi-sweet chocolate
100 gm .	4 oz	sugar
5 tsp .	2 tbsp	cornflour
		whipped cream

Cut sponge cakes into thin slices. Mix two-thirds of the milk with the chocolate in top of double saucepan over hot water and stir until melted and smooth. Blend sugar and cornflour with remaining milk and stir into chocolate mixture. Continue cooking and stirring until thickened. Layer one-quarter of sponge cake slices in a loaf tin and pour one-third of chocolate mixture over. Repeat layers, ending with cake, pressing down firmly. Chill several hours. Unmould and ice top and sides with whipped cream.

BRANDIED FRUIT POT

4 675-gm tins		
	4 24-oz tins	fruit salad, drained
450 gm .	1 lb	sugar
275 ml .	½ pt	brandy

Mix well and put in a large crock or jar. Cover with a plate or saucer. DO NOT USE A TIGHT-FITTING LID. Allow to stand at *room* temperature. Replace as used by adding one large tin fruit, drained, and 4 oz (115 gm) sugar. The mixture ferments, creating its own 'brandy' which acts as a preservative. It will keep indefinitely. Do not allow mixture to get much below 1 qt (1 l.). Use as a topping for ice cream or cake.

Cobblers and Pies

SHORTCRUST	*300 gm* . 12 oz	plain flour
PASTRY	pinch	salt
	150 gm . 6 oz	cooking fat or lard
	5-6 tbsp . 6-7 tbsp	cold water

Mix flour and salt. Cut fat into flour with a pastry blender or two knives, or work it in with fingers until well blended and the texture of fine crumbs. Mix in enough water to form a stiff dough. Halve. Roll out on a floured board.

Double-Crust Pie

Cut a circle of pastry slightly larger than pie plate. Place in pie plate and pour the filling into it. Cut remaining pastry to fit top, cover filling, and seal and crimp edges between thumb and forefinger. Cut several small slits in top of crust, or prick with a fork. Bake as recipe directs.

Single-Crust Pie

Prepare half of recipe for Shortcrust Pastry and cut to fit pie plate. Crimp the edge.

Baked Crust

Prepare Single-Crust Pie. With a fork punch several holes in bottom of crust. Press a piece of foil firmly inside and bake in a moderately hot oven (425° F, 220° C, Gas Mark 7) for 10 minutes. (If foil puffs up during baking, press down with potholder.) Remove foil and bake 5 minutes longer or until lightly browned. Cool.

COOKIE CRUMB CRUST	100 gm . 4 oz	sweetmeal biscuits, finely crushed
	2 tbsp	sugar
	50 gm . 2 oz	butter, melted

Crush the biscuits with a rolling pin until crumbs are very fine. Mix with the sugar. Melt butter and stir in the crumbs. Spread over bottom and sides of a 9-in. (23-cm) pie plate, pressing firmly with back of spoon. Chill. Use in place of Baked Crust.

APPLE PIE		shortcrust pastry for double-crust pie
	900 gm . 2 lb	cooking apples, sliced
	170 gm . 6 oz	sugar
	2 tbsp	plain flour
	½ tsp	cinnamon
	¼ tsp	nutmeg
	dash	salt
	2 tbsp	butter
		sugar

Prepare pastry and line 9-in. (23-cm) pie plate. Mix apples, sugar, flour, cinnamon, nutmeg and salt and pile into pastry. Dot with butter and cover with top crust. Seal and flute edge and prick with fork in several places. Sprinkle top of crust with sugar. Bake in a hot oven (450°F, 230°C, Gas Mark 8) for 10 minutes. Lower heat (350°F, 180°C, Gas Mark 4) and bake until apples are tender (about 30 minutes).

DEEP DISH APPLE PIE	900 gm . 2 lb	cooking apples, peeled, cored and sliced
	170 gm . 6 oz	sugar
	4 tbsp	flour
	½ tsp	nutmeg
	½ tsp	cinnamon
	¼ tsp	salt
		shortcrust pastry for single-crust pie

Combine apples, sugar, flour, spices and salt and turn into buttered oven-proof dish. Prepare pastry and roll to fit top of dish. Cut several small slits in pastry and fit over dish, crimping edges with fingers. Bake in hot oven (450°F, 230°C, Gas Mark 8) for 10 minutes. Lower heat (350°F, 180°C, Gas Mark 4) and bake 30 minutes longer. Serve warm with cream or ice cream.
Serves 6.

APPLE	900 gm . 2 lb	cooking apples, peeled
COBBLER	170 gm . 6 oz	sugar
	2 tbsp	plain flour
	½ tsp	cinnamon
	½ tsp	nutmeg
	¼ tsp	salt
Crust	100 gm . 4 oz	plain flour
	1 tsp	baking powder
	¼ tsp	salt
	2½ tbsp . 3 tbsp	cooking fat
	1	egg yolk
	3½ tbsp . 4 tbsp	milk

Combine apples, sugar, flour, spices and salt and turn into buttered oven-proof dish. Prepare crust: sieve flour, baking powder and salt and rub in fat. Beat egg yolk and mix with milk. Add to flour mixture and mix well. Roll out to fit dish and lay on top of apple mixture. Bake in a moderate oven (350°F, 180°C, Gas Mark 4) for 30 minutes. Serve warm.

HARVEST FRUIT	400 gm . 1 lb	cooking apples
COBBLER	100 gm . 4 oz	dried figs
	100 gm . 4 oz	dried apricots
	50 gm . 2 oz	raisins
	75 gm . 3 oz	sugar
	¼ tsp	cinnamon
	¼ tsp	ginger
	¼ tsp	nutmeg
	1½ tbsp . 2 tbsp	plain flour
	2½ tsp . 1 tbsp	butter
		crust as for Apple Cobbler

Peel, core and chop apples. Chop figs and apricots. Combine fruits, sugar, spices, flour and add 1 gill (125 ml) water. Mix well and cook, stirring, over low heat until mixture thickens. Cool slightly and pour into a buttered oven-proof dish. Prepare crust as for Apple Cobbler and spread over top. Bake in a moderate oven (350°F, 180°C, Gas Mark 4) for 30 minutes. Serve warm.
   Serves 6.

CUSTARD PIE		shortcrust pastry for single-crust pie
	4	eggs
	115 gm . 4 oz	sugar
	¼ tsp	salt
	550 ml . 1 pt	milk
	½ tsp	vanilla essence
	¼ tsp	nutmeg

Prepare pastry and line a 9-in. (23-cm) pie plate. Mix eggs with sugar and salt. Stir in milk gradually. Add vanilla and pour into pastry-lined plate. Sprinkle with nutmeg and bake in a hot oven (450°F, 230°C, Gas Mark 8) for 10 minutes. Reduce heat (325°F, 170°C, Gas Mark 3) and bake until filling is set (about 25 minutes). Cool.

LEMON MERINGUE PIE

		shortcrust pastry for single-crust pie, baked
	3 tbsp	cornflour
200 gm .	7 oz	sugar
	¼ tsp	salt
	3	egg yolks
275 ml .	½ pt	water
	1 large	lemon (juice and grated rind)
	3	egg whites
	4 tbsp	sugar

Prepare shortcrust pastry and line a 9-in. (23-cm) pie plate. Bake and cool. Mix cornflour, sugar, egg yolks and salt in a saucepan. Gradually add water, lemon juice and rind. Cook over low heat, stirring continually, until mixture is thick. Set aside. Beat egg whites until stiff and beat in sugar 1 tablespoon at a time. Mixture should stand in stiff peaks. Pour lemon mixture into baked cooled crust and spread meringue over it, covering completely. Bake in a moderate oven (350°F, 180°C, Gas Mark 4) until pale gold. Cool completely before cutting.

GRASSHOPPER PIE

100 gm .	4 oz	sweetmeal biscuits, finely crushed
	2 tbsp	cocoa
	2 tbsp	sugar
	4 tbsp	butter, melted
225 gm .	8 oz	marshmallows
140 ml .	1 gill	milk
	3 tbsp	green crème de menthe
350 ml .	⅔ pt	double cream

To Decorate

275 ml .	½ pt	double cream, whipped
	2 tbsp	shaved chocolate

Blend biscuit crumbs, cocoa and sugar with melted butter. Press over bottom and sides of 9-in. (23-cm) pie plate. Chill.

Place marshmallows and milk in top of double saucepan over hot water and stir until melted and blended. Cool. Stir in crème de menthe. Beat cream until stiff and fold into marshmallow mixture. Spoon into crust and chill several hours. Before serving top with ring of whipped cream and sprinkle shaved chocolate over all.

STRAWBERRY GLAZE PIE

		shortcrust pastry for single-crust pie, baked
565 gm .	20 oz	frozen sliced strawberries, thawed
115 gm .	4 oz	sugar
		cornflour
	2 tsp	lemon juice
275 ml .	½ pt	thick cream
	2 tbsp	sugar

Prepare and bake crust in a 9-in. (23-cm) pie plate. Cool. Mix sugar with thawed berries and place in a strainer. Measure juice and add 1 tablespoon cornflour for each gill (140 ml) of juice. Stir to dissolve and add lemon juice. Cook, stirring, over medium heat until thickened. Cool. Spread sliced berries evenly in baked cooled crust and pour thickened juice over them. Whip cream with 2 tablespoons sugar and spread over top of pie.

FRENCH APPLE PIE

		shortcrust pastry for single-crust pie
800 gm .	2 lb	cooking apples
100 gm .	4 oz	sugar
	⅛ tsp	cinnamon

Topping

75 gm .	3 oz	plain flour
125 gm .	5 oz	sugar
	¼ tsp	salt
	⅛ tsp	cinnamon
100 gm .	4 oz	butter

Prepare pastry and line a 9-in. (23-cm) pie plate. Peel, core and slice apples and combine with sugar and cinnamon. Prepare Topping: sieve flour, sugar, salt and cinnamon and rub in butter. Sprinkle over the apple filling. Bake in a moderately hot oven (425°F, 220°C, Gas Mark 7) for 15 minutes. Reduce heat (350°F, 180°C, Gas Mark 4) and bake 25 minutes. Serve warm or cold.

BANANA CREAM PIE

		shortcrust pastry for single-crust pie, baked, *or* Cookie Crumb Crust
550 ml .	1 pt	milk
	3	egg yolks
	3 tbsp	cornflour
	¼ tsp	salt
115 gm .	4 oz	sugar
	1 tsp	vanilla essence
	3	bananas, sliced
275 ml .	½ pt	double cream
	2 tbsp	sugar

well with a spoon. Bake in a moderate oven (350°F, 180°C, Gas Mark 4) for 30 minutes.

COCONUT-	100 gm . 4 oz	butter
BROWN SUGAR	200 gm . 8 oz	brown sugar
ICING	65 ml . ½ gill	evaporated milk
	300 gm . 12 oz	icing sugar
	50 gm . 2 oz	desiccated coconut
	50 gm . 2 oz	chopped nuts

Melt butter and add brown sugar. Cook over medium heat, stirring, until mixture boils. Boil 2 minutes. Remove from heat and add milk. Stir in icing sugar and beat until smooth. Blend in coconut and nuts.

German Chocolate Cake

Prepare Devil's Food Cake but spread Coconut-Brown Sugar Icing between layers and over top and sides.

MARSHMALLOW	275 ml . ½ pt	light corn syrup
FROSTING	2	egg whites
	pinch	salt

Bring syrup to boil. Set aside. Beat egg whites and salt until mixture holds shape. Continue beating while pouring hot syrup slowly into egg whites. Beat until very stiff.

Cookies

OATMEAL
RAISIN COOKIES

150 gm .	6 oz	butter or margarine
100 gm .	4 oz	brown sugar
75 gm .	3 oz	granulated sugar
	1	egg
3½ tbsp .	4 tbsp	milk
200 gm .	8 oz	quick-cooking oats
100 gm .	4 oz	plain flour
	½ tsp	bicarbonate of soda
¾ tsp .	1 tsp	cinnamon
	¼ tsp	cloves
	¼ tsp	salt
50 gm .	2 oz	chopped nuts
100 gm .	4 oz	raisins

Cream butter and sugars. Beat in egg. Add milk and blend well. Combine remaining ingredients and stir in. Drop by teaspoonfuls onto greased baking sheet and bake in a moderate oven (375° F, 190° C, Gas Mark 5) until lightly browned (10-12 minutes).
5 dozen.

BROWN SUGAR
BARS

50 gm .	2 oz	butter or margarine
175 gm .	7 oz	brown sugar
	1	egg, beaten
	1 tsp	vanilla essence
5 tsp .	2 tbsp	milk
100 gm .	4 oz	plain flour
	1 tsp	baking powder
	¼ tsp	salt
	½ tsp	cinnamon
	¼ tsp	nutmeg
50 gm .	2 oz	raisins

Melt butter in a saucepan, add sugar and stir over heat until bubbly. Allow to cool. Combine egg, vanilla essence and milk and add to sugar mixture. Sieve flour, baking powder, salt and spices and stir into the batter. Add raisins and spread in a buttered 9-in. (23-cm) square baking tin. Bake in a moderate oven (350° F, 180° C, Gas Mark 4) for 20-25 minutes. Cool slightly and cut into bars.
About 3 dozen.

BROWNIES

100 gm .	4 oz	butter or margarine
175 gm .	7 oz	sugar
	2	eggs
	1 tsp	vanilla essence
50 gm .	2 oz	unsweetened chocolate
75 gm .	3 oz	plain flour
	½ tsp	baking powder
	¼ tsp	salt
50 gm .	2 oz	chopped nuts
		Chocolate Icing (optional)

Cream butter and sugar together and beat in eggs and vanilla. Melt chocolate and add to mixture. Combine flour, baking powder and salt and stir in, blending well. Add nuts. Spread mixture in a buttered 8-in. (20-cm) square baking tin and bake in a moderate oven (350° F, 180° C, Gas Mark 4) for 30-35 minutes. Cool in tin and ice with Chocolate Icing, if desired. Cut into squares.

CHOCOLATE CHIP COOKIES

150 gm .	6 oz	butter or margarine
75 gm .	3 oz	brown sugar
100 gm .	4 oz	granulated sugar
	1	egg
	1 tsp	vanilla essence
200 gm .	8 oz	plain flour
	½ tsp	bicarbonate of soda
	¼ tsp	salt
50 gm .	2 oz	chopped nuts
150 gm .	6 oz	semi-sweet chocolate pieces

Cream butter and sugars thoroughly. Beat in egg and vanilla. Mix flour, soda, salt, nuts and chocolate pieces and stir into batter. Drop by teaspoonfuls onto ungreased baking sheet and bake in a moderate oven (375° F, 190° C, Gas Mark 5) until lightly browned (8-10 minutes). Wait a few seconds before removing from baking sheet.

5 dozen.

Choco-Mint Cookies

Use 1 teaspoon peppermint essence and 2 oz (50 gm) of desiccated coconut and omit vanilla and nuts in above recipe.

NO-BAKE	175 gm . 7 oz	sugar
CHOCOLATE	25 gm . 1 oz	semi-sweet chocolate
OATMEAL	50 gm . 2 oz	butter
COOKIES	3½ tbsp . 4 tbsp	evaporated milk
	½ tsp	almond essence
	115 gm . 4½ oz	quick-cooking oatmeal
	40 gm . 1½ oz	desiccated coconut
	25 gm . 1 oz	chopped nuts

Combine sugar, chocolate, butter and milk in saucepan and boil one minute. Add almond. Mix oats, coconut and nuts and combine well with chocolate mixture. Drop by teaspoonfuls onto buttered baking sheet. Cool.

MOLASSES	100 gm . 4 oz	butter or margarine
(TREACLE)	65 gm . 2½ oz	brown sugar
COOKIES	1	egg
	7 tbsp . 8 tbsp	treacle
	3½ tbsp . 4 tbsp	milk
	200 gm . 8 oz	plain flour
	¼ tsp	salt
	½ tsp	ginger
	½ tsp	cinnamon
	1 tsp	bicarbonate of soda

Cream butter and sugar together. Beat in egg. Add treacle and milk and mix thoroughly. Sieve flour, salt, spices and soda together and combine with mixture. Drop by heaping teaspoonfuls onto buttered baking sheet and bake in a moderate oven (375°F, 190°C, Gas Mark 5) for about 10 minutes.

About 4 dozen.

Breads and Rolls

BAKING POWDER BISCUITS

200 gm .	8 oz	plain flour
2½ tsp .	3 tsp	baking powder
	1 tsp	salt
4½ tbsp .	5 tbsp	salad oil
125 ml .	1 gill	milk

Sieve flour, baking powder and salt. Mix oil with milk and stir into flour mixture. On floured board, roll or pat dough to ¾-in. (2-cm) thickness. Using a floured cutter or a tumbler dipped in flour, cut biscuits into small rounds and place on a greased baking sheet. Bake in a hot oven (450°F, 230°C, Gas Mark 8) for 10-12 minutes or until browned. Serve hot with butter and jam.
12 — 15 biscuits.

ZUCCHINI BREAD

300 gm .	12 oz	courgettes, peeled and grated
100 gm .	4 oz	butter or margarine
100 gm .	4 oz	sugar
125 gm .	5 oz	honey
	2	eggs
250 gm .	10 oz	plain flour
	1 tsp	bicarbonate of soda
	½ tsp	cinnamon
	½ tsp	nutmeg
	¼ tsp	salt
75 gm .	3 oz	chopped nuts
50 gm .	2 oz	raisins

Cream butter with sugar. Beat in eggs and honey. Sieve flour with soda, cinnamon, nutmeg and salt and add to first mixture. Add grated courgettes, nuts and raisins, and mix well. Pour into a greased loaf tin and bake in a moderate oven (350°F, 180°C, Gas Mark 4) for 75 minutes. Cool in tin. Wait at least 12 hours before slicing.

TEA MUFFINS

175 gm.	7 oz	plain flour
2¼ tsp .	2½ tsp	baking powder
	½ tsp	salt
2½ tbsp .	3 tbsp	sugar
	1	egg, beaten
125 ml .	1 gill	milk
3½ tbsp .	4 tbsp	salad oil

Sieve together flour, baking powder, salt and sugar. Combine egg, milk and oil and add to flour mixture. Stir just until blended and pour into greased patty tins (two-thirds full). Bake in a moderately hot oven (400° F, 200° C, Gas Mark 6) for 25 minutes. Serve warm with butter.

Raisin-Spice Muffins

Add 2 oz (50 gm) raisins, ½ tsp cinnamon and ½ tsp nutmeg to above recipe.

APPLESAUCE BREAD

250 ml . ½ pt	applesauce
100 gm . 4 oz	butter or margarine, melted
2	eggs
225 gm . 9 oz	plain flour
1 tsp	bicarbonate of soda
¾ tsp	salt
1 tsp	ginger
½ tsp . ¾ tsp	cinnamon
¾ tsp . 1 tsp	nutmeg
125 gm . 5 oz	sugar
75 gm . 3 oz	raisins

Mix applesauce, melted butter and eggs together. Combine flour, soda, salt, spices, sugar and raisins and pour into the applesauce mixture. Stir until blended. Turn into greased loaf tin and bake in a moderate oven (350° F, 180° C, Gas Mark 4) for 65 minutes.

OATMEAL MUFFINS

150 gm . 6 oz	plain flour
50 gm . 2 oz	sugar
1¾ tsp . 2 tsp	baking powder
1 tsp	salt
75 gm . 3 oz	oatmeal
165 ml . ⅓ pt	milk
1	egg, beaten
3½ tbsp . 4 tbsp	honey or golden syrup
50 gm . 2 oz	butter or margarine, melted
75 gm . 3 oz	raisins

Combine flour, sugar, baking powder, salt and oatmeal. Mix milk with egg, honey and melted butter and stir into flour mixture. Add raisins and pour into 12 greased patty tins (two-thirds full). Bake in a moderately hot oven (400° F, 200° C, Gas Mark 6) for 20 minutes. Serve warm with butter.

BRAN MUFFINS

50 gm .	2 oz	plain flour
75 gm .	3 oz	wholemeal flour
65 gm .	2½ oz	bran
5 tsp .	2 tbsp	sugar
	⅛ tsp	salt
1 tsp .	1¼ tsp	bicarbonate of soda
250 ml .	½ pt	milk
	1	egg, beaten
65 ml .	½ gill	treacle
2½ tbsp .	3 tbsp	margarine, melted

Combine flours, bran, sugar, salt and soda. Mix milk, egg, treacle and melted margarine and pour into the flour mixture. Stir until blended. Pour into 12 greased patty tins (two-thirds full) and bake in a moderate oven (350°F, 180°C, Gas Mark 4) for 20-25 minutes. Serve warm with butter.

BASIC SWEET ROLL DOUGH

200 ml .	1½ gills	milk
170 gm .	6 oz	butter or margarine, melted
85 gm .	3 oz	sugar
7 gm .	¼ oz	active dry yeast
	5 tbsp	lukewarm water
675 gm .	1½ lb	plain flour
	2	eggs
	½ tsp	salt

Heat milk to scalding, add butter and stir in sugar until dissolved. Cool until lukewarm. Dissolve yeast in lukewarm water and leave to stand 5 minutes. Combine yeast mixture with milk in a large basin and add one-third of the flour. Beat until smooth. Leave to stand in a warm place 10 minutes. Beat eggs with salt and add to batter. Add three-quarters of remaining flour, a little at a time, mixing well after each addition. Pour remaining flour onto a board and turn the dough onto it. Knead until smooth and elastic (about 8 minutes), working in extra flour only as required to prevent stickiness. Place dough in a clean greased basin, turning to grease all surfaces.* Cover and leave to rise in a warm place until doubled. Divide into two equal portions and use in any recipe calling for Basic Sweet Roll Dough.

*When making Christmas Stollen, omit this last step and proceed according to recipe.

BUTTERHORNS

Basic Sweet Roll Dough recipe — halve quantities
2 tbsp   butter

Roll into two 9-in. (23-cm) circles and cut each into 12 wedges. Roll up each wedge from the wide end. Lay on a buttered baking sheet and cover with a clean towel. Allow to rise again in a warm place until double. Brush tops with melted butter and bake in a hot oven (425°F, 220°C, Gas Mark 7) for about 15 minutes.

MAPLE BARS

Basic Sweet Roll Dough recipe halve quantities (see p. 187)
2 tbsp   melted butter

Roll dough to ¾-in. (2-cm) thickness. Cut into bars 4 in. (10 cm) long by 1½ in. (4 cm) wide. Place bars on buttered baking sheet, with space between. Cover with clean towel and leave to rise in a warm place until doubled in bulk. Brush tops with melted butter and bake in a moderately hot oven (400°F, 200°C, Gas Mark 6) 20-25 minutes. Ice with Maple Icing.

Maple Icing

225 gm	8 oz	icing sugar
	pinch	salt
	1 tbsp	butter
	3 tbsp	maple syrup or dark corn syrup
	1 tbsp	cream

Beat together until well blended.

FRENCH TOAST

	2	eggs
180 ml	⅓ pt	milk
	¼ tsp	salt
	6	slices white bread
	2 tbsp	cooking fat or oil

Beat eggs, add milk and salt and beat well. Pour into shallow dish. Place a slice of bread in mixture and wait a few seconds for it to absorb. Life out carefully and fry in hot oil until golden-brown on both sides. Serve hot with butter and syrup.

Cinnamon French Toast

Prepare French Toast as above but instead of serving with butter and syrup, sprinkle with cinnamon and sugar.

GARLIC BREAD	1 loaf	French bread
	2 cloves	garlic, crushed
	8 tbsp	butter

Cut loaf not quite through to the bottom, making the cuts ¾ in. (2 cm) apart. Mash garlic and butter together and spread mixture on one side of each cut. Push slices together and place loaf on a baking sheet. Bake in a moderately hot oven (400°F, 200°C, Gas Mark 6) for 10 minutes. Serve hot.

PARMESAN	6 small	hard-crusted rolls
BREAD	6 tbsp	butter
	2 tbsp	grated Parmesan cheese

Split rolls and spread with butter. Sprinkle the cheese over the butter and put rolls on a baking sheet. Place under a heated grill until golden-brown and crisp. Serve hot.

GARLIC TOAST	6 small	hard-crusted rolls
	6 tbsp	butter
	¼ tsp	powdered garlic

Cut rolls in half. Mix butter and garlic and spread over cut sides of rolls. Place on baking sheet and place under a hot grill until golden-brown and crisp. Serve hot.

CHEESE BREAD	4 tbsp	butter
	30 gm . 1 oz	grated Cheddar cheese
	12 gm . ½ oz	grated Parmesan cheese
	⅛ tsp	Worcestershire sauce
	dash	pepper
	4 slices	white sandwich bread

Mash butter, cheeses, Worcestershire sauce and pepper together thoroughly. Spread on slices of bread and toast under the grill.

CINNAMON		sliced white bread
TOAST		butter
		cinnamon
		sugar

Toast bread slices under a grill on one side only. Spread the untoasted side with butter, sprinkle with cinnamon and then with sugar. Return to the grill until top is browned and crisp.

Sandwiches

BACON AND TOMATO SANDWICH

6 rashers	streaky bacon
2	tomatoes, sliced
4	lettuce leaves
	mayonnaise
8 slices	bread, toasted

Cut bacon slices in halves and fry until crisp; drain on paper towels. Spread toast lightly with mayonnaise. On each of four slices toast lay three pieces of bacon, cover with sliced tomato, a lettuce leaf, and remaining toast. Serve immediately.

4 sandwiches.

CLUB SANDWICHES

9 slices	bread
2 tbsp	butter
3 slices	roast chicken or turkey
6 rashers	streaky bacon, fried crisp
2 tbsp	mayonnaise
1 large	tomato, sliced
3	lettuce leaves
	salt, pepper

Toast bread and spread six slices with butter. On three of buttered slices lay chicken and bacon, three more slices of buttered toast (buttered side down) spread with half of mayonnaise, add sliced tomato, lettuce leaves, and sprinkle with salt and pepper. Spread remaining toast slices with mayonnaise and place on top. To hold sandwiches firmly stick wooden toothpick in each corner. Cut diagonally into quarters.

3 sandwiches.

SUBMARINES

4	hot dog rolls
	butter
2 tbsp	mayonnaise
100 gm . 4 oz	boiled ham
4 thin slices	cheese
125 gm . 4 oz	salami
2	tomatoes, sliced
4	lettuce leaves

Split rolls and spread bottom halves with butter and tops with mayonnaise. On buttered halves pile thinly sliced ham, cheese, salami, tomatoes and lettuce, and cover with top halves of rolls.

4 sandwiches.

TOASTED	6 slices	bread, buttered
CHEESE	3 slices	cheese
SANDWICHES		

Place three slices of bread, butter side down, in cold frying pan. Place cheese slices on bread and cover with remaining bread slices, butter side up. Fry gently until bottoms are golden-brown. Turn carefully and fry until other side is brown and cheese is melted.

3 sandwiches.

BARBECUED	170 gm . 4 oz	cooked ham
HAM	4 tbsp	ketchup
SANDWICHES	1 tbsp	vinegar
	2 tsp	brown sugar
	¼ tsp	pepper
	1 tbsp	water
	2	hamburger buns, split and toasted

Cut ham into small thin pieces. Mix ketchup, vinegar, brown sugar, pepper and water and bring to boil. Add ham and simmer 5 minutes, stirring frequently. Serve hot between halves of buns.

2 sandwiches.

Barbecued Beef Sandwiches

Substitute cooked roast beef for ham in above recipe.

Beverages

COFFEE

1 l.	. 1 qt	cold water
3½ tbsp	. 4 tbsp	ground coffee
		paper filter or white
		facial tissue
		cream, sugar

Electric coffee pot: Follow manufacturer's directions for use, but use proportions above, and place a paper filter in the coffee basket. A facial tissue may be used as a filter if a small hole is made in the centre; fold corners up over coffee.

Percolator: Place cold water in coffee pot, place a filter in the basket before adding coffee. Place over medium heat until coffee begins to 'perk'. Turn to low and allow to perk gently 10-15 minutes. NEVER ALLOW COFFEE TO BOIL.

Dripolator: Bring water to boil in kettle. Place coffee in basket over empty coffee pot and pour boiling water slowly into top part of dripolator. As soon as coffee has dripped through it is ready to serve.

MOCHA

4 heaped tsp	cocoa
4 heaped tsp	sugar
1 pt	hot coffee
275 ml . ½ pt	hot milk

Mix cocoa and sugar and add a little of the hot coffee. Mix well and add remaining coffee and hot milk. Stir and serve immediately.
   Serves 4.

ICED MOCHA

Prepare Hot Mocha and allow to cool. Fill tall glasses with ice cubes and pour Mocha over them.

SPICED TEA

1 l.	1 qt	boiling water
4½ tsp	5 tsp	tea leaves
7	8	whole cloves
100 gm	4 oz	sugar
5 tsp	2 tbsp	lemon juice
125 ml	1 gill	orange juice

Pour boiling water over leaves and cloves. Allow to stand 5 minutes. Strain into saucepan. Add sugar and juices and heat to boiling. Serve hot.

5 — 6 servings.

Index

White Glaze Icing, 99
White Sauce, 157
Wiener Boats, 146-7

Yams, Hawaiian-Style, 73